BIG-NOTE PIANO

2nd EDITION

ELTON JOHN
GREATEST HITS

ISBN 978-0-7935-4626-8

HAL•LEONARD®
CORPORATION

7777 W. BLUEMOUND RD. P.O. BOX 13819 MILWAUKEE, WI 53213

Visit Hal Leonard Online at
www.halleonard.com

BENNIE AND THE JETS

Words and Music by ELTON JOHN
and BERNIE TAUPIN

Hey kids, shake it loose to-geth-er the spot-
Hey kids, plug in-to the faith-less may-

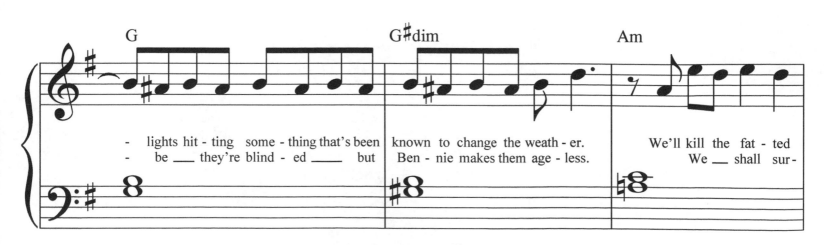

- lights hit-ting some-thing that's been   known to change the weath-er.   We'll kill the fat-ted
- be __ they're blind-ed __ but   Ben-nie makes them age-less.   We __ shall sur-

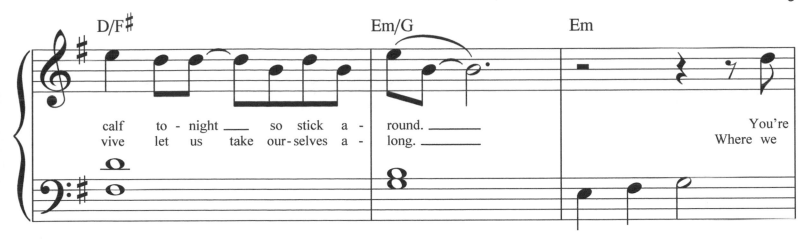

D/F♯   Em/G   Em

calf   to - night ___ so stick a - round. ___   You're
vive   let us take our-selves a - long. ___   Where we

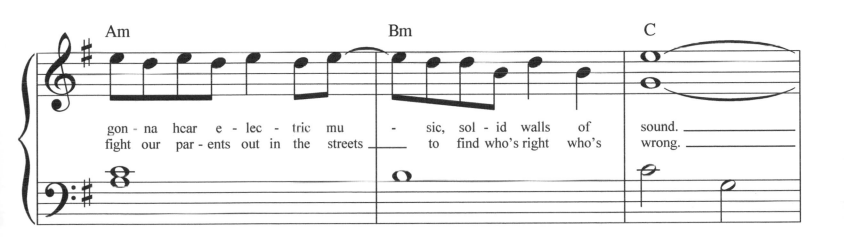

Am   Bm   C

gon - na hear e - lec - tric mu - sic, sol - id walls of sound. ___
fight our par - ents out in the streets ___ to find who's right who's wrong. ___

G

Say,   Can - dy and Ron — nie have you seen them yet but

Am   5   2   C

they're   so spaced   out, ___   Ben - nie and the Jets. ___

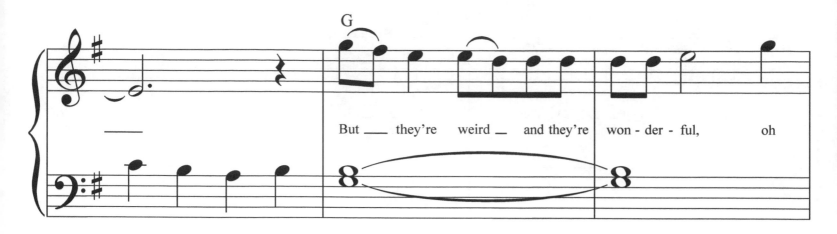

But — they're weird — and they're won - der - ful, oh

Ben - nie, she's — real - ly keen. She's got e - lec - tric boots, a

mo - hair suit, — you know I read it in a mag - a - zine — oh, —

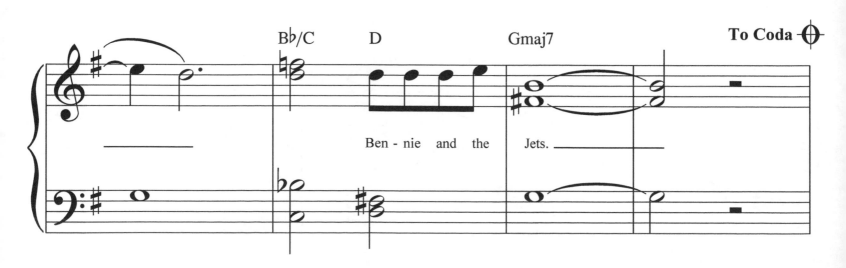

Ben - nie and the Jets. —

To Coda

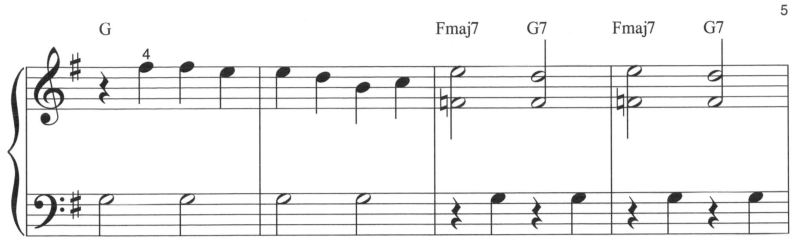

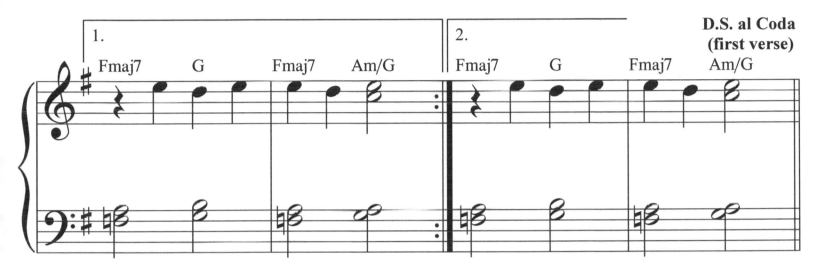

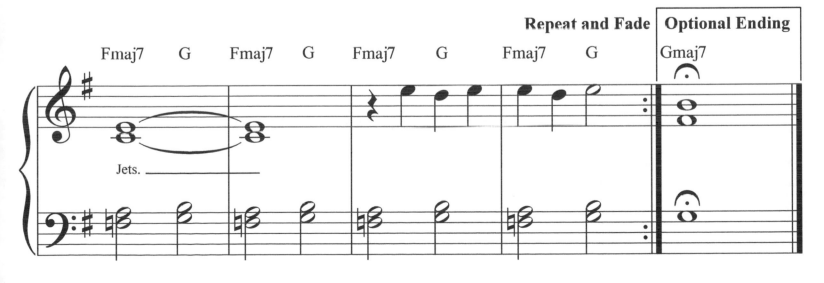

DON'T GO BREAKING MY HEART

Words and Music by CARTE BLANCHE
and ANN ORSON

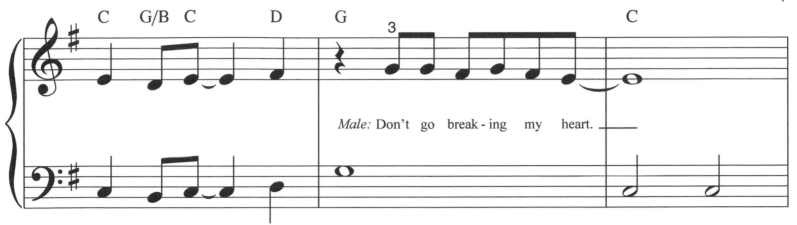

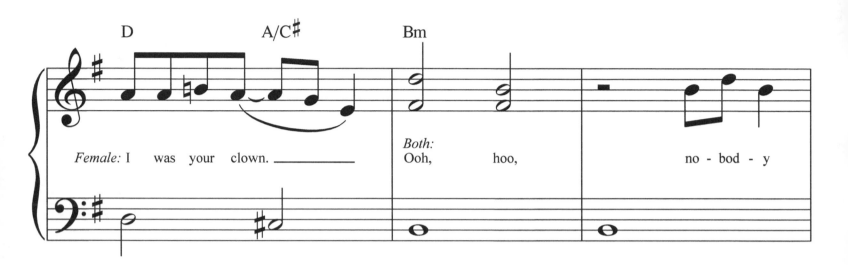

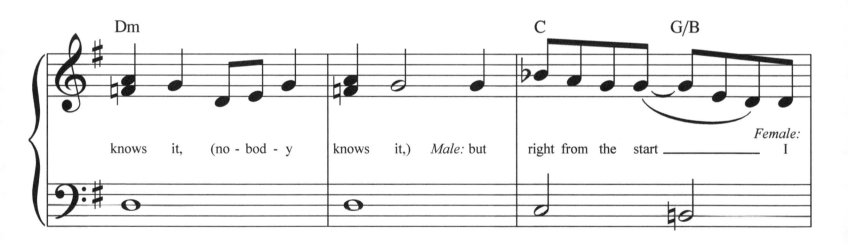

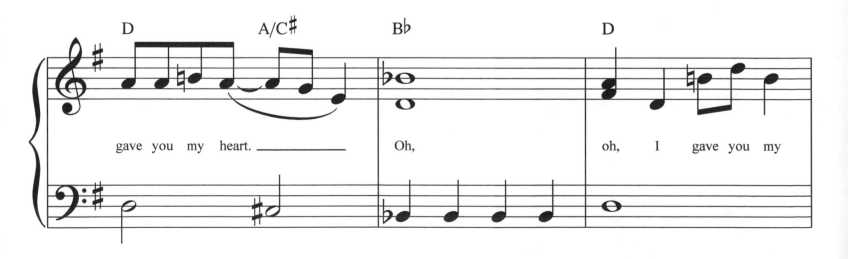

10

Additional Lyrics

Male: And nobody told us
Female: 'Cause nobody showed us.
Male: And now it's up to us, babe.
Female: Oh, I think we can make it.
Male: So don't misunderstand me.
Female: You put the light in my life.
Male: Oh, you put the spark in my flame.
Female: I've got your heart in my sights.

CAN YOU FEEL THE LOVE TONIGHT

from Walt Disney Pictures' THE LION KING

Music by ELTON JOHN
Lyrics by TIM RICE

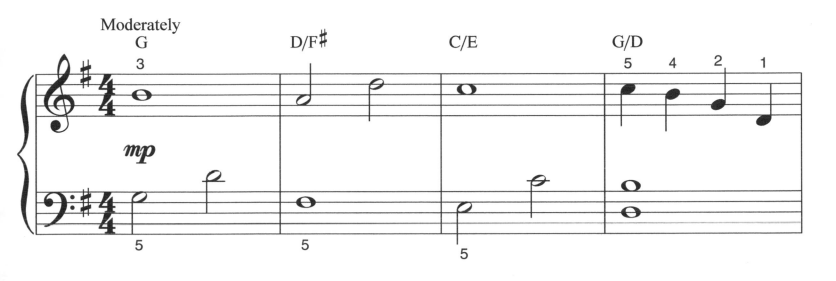

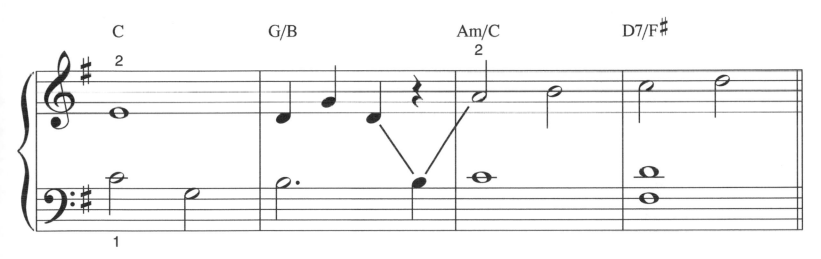

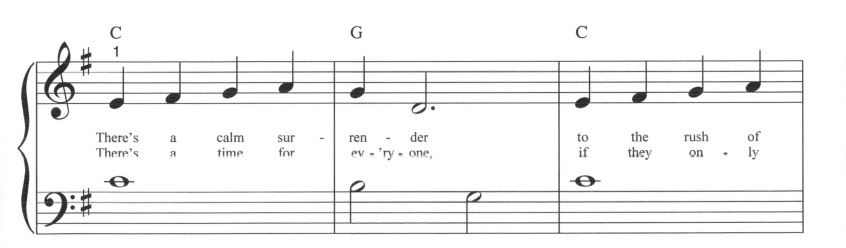

There's a calm sur - ren - der to the rush of
There's a time for ev - 'ry - one, if they on - ly

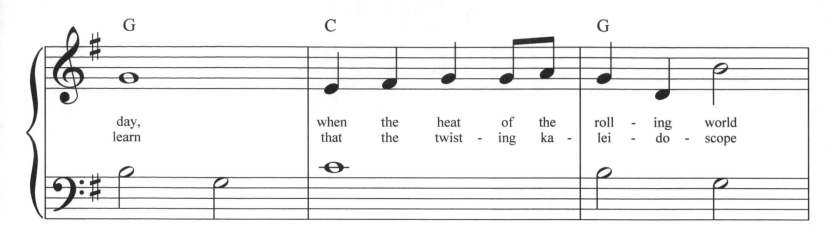

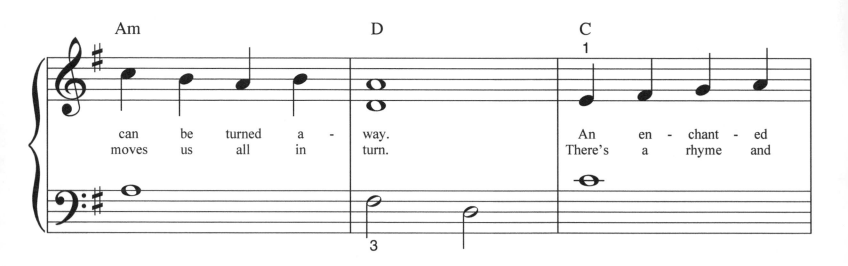

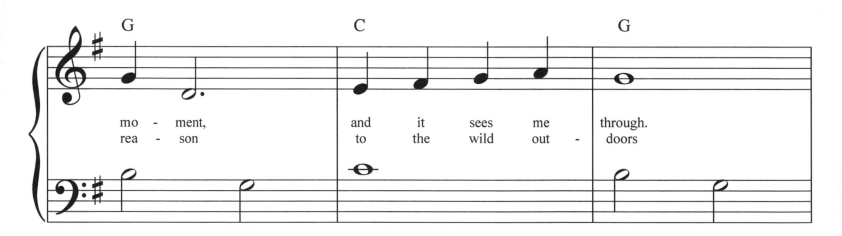

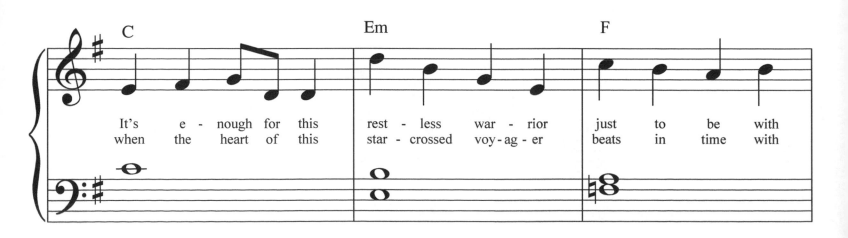

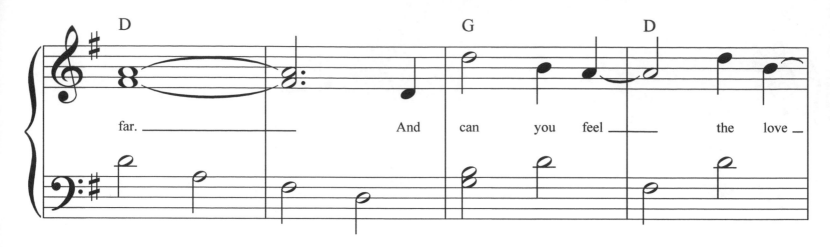

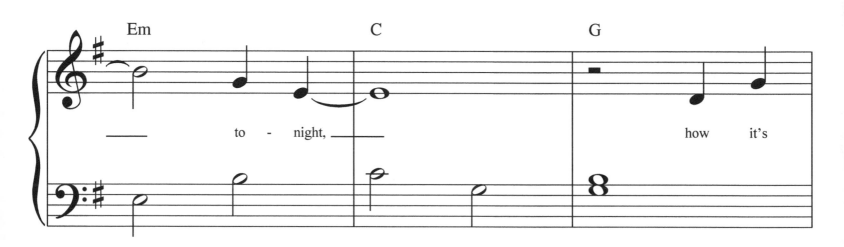

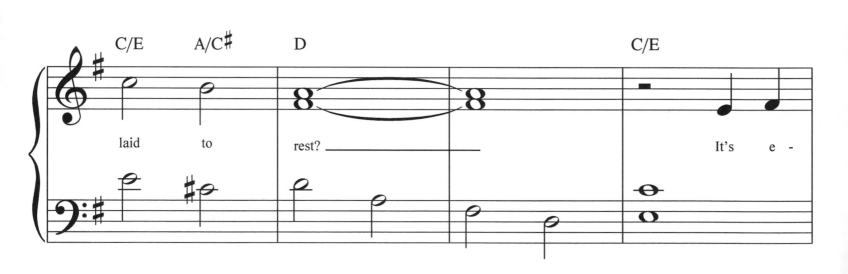

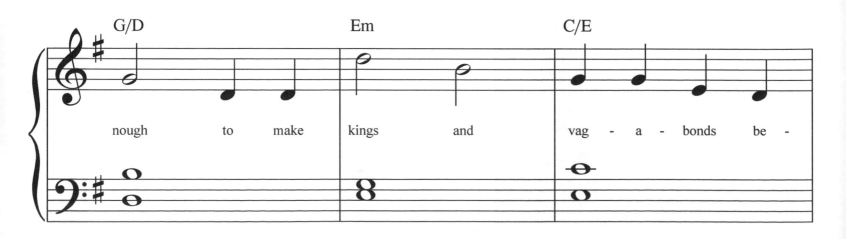

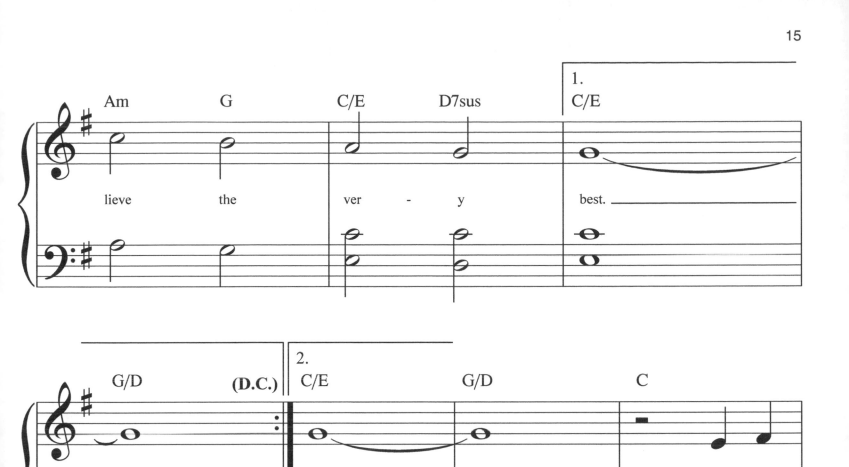

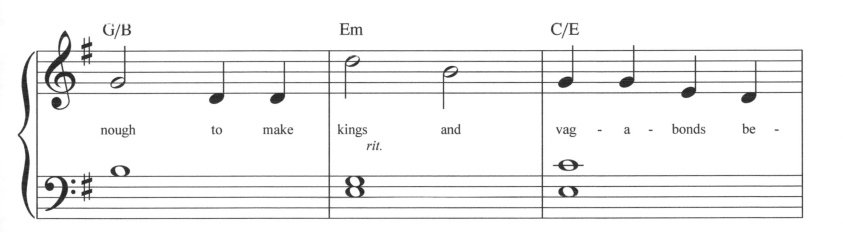

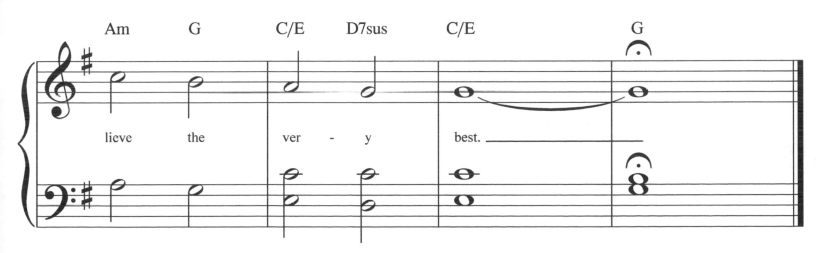

CANDLE IN THE WIND

Words and Music by ELTON JOHN
and BERNIE TAUPIN

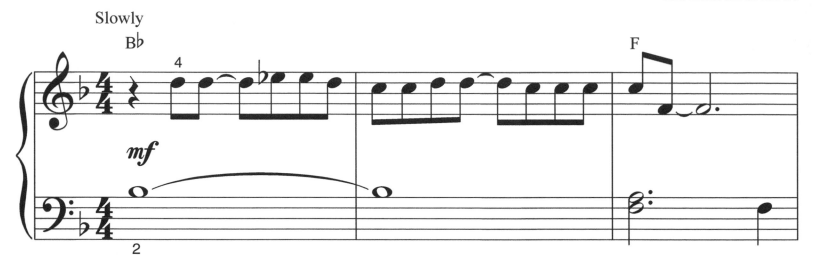

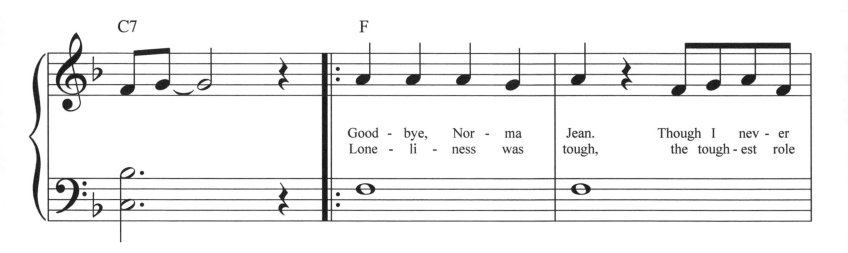

Good - bye, Nor - ma Jean. Though I nev - er
Lone - li - ness was tough, the tough - est role

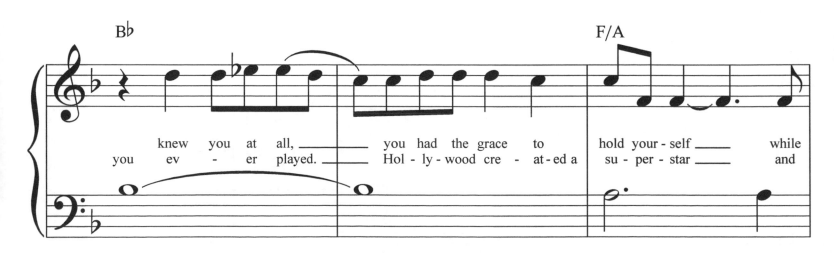

knew you at all, _____ you had the grace to hold your - self _____ while
you ev - er played. _____ Hol - ly - wood cre - at - ed a su - per - star _____ and

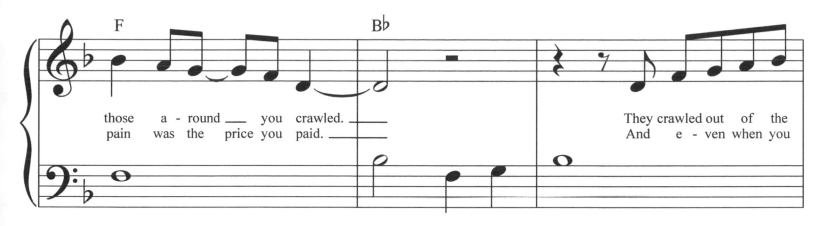

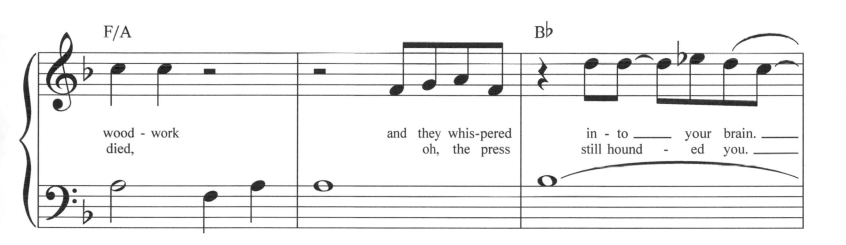

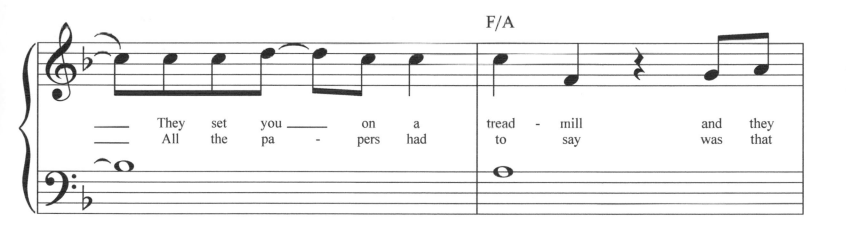

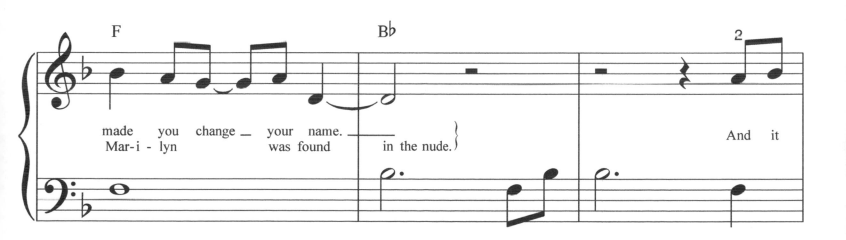

seems to me ___ you lived your life ___ like a can - dle in ___ the

wind, nev - er know - ing who to cling to when the rain set in. ___

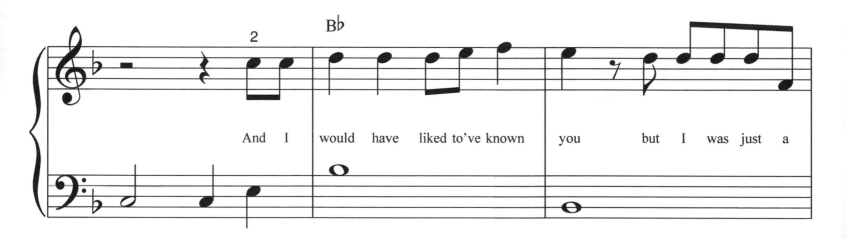

And I would have liked to've known you but I was just a

kid. Your can - dle burned out long ___ be - fore ___

To Coda

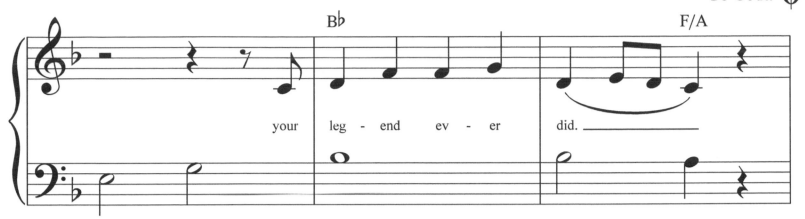

your leg - end ev - er did. _____

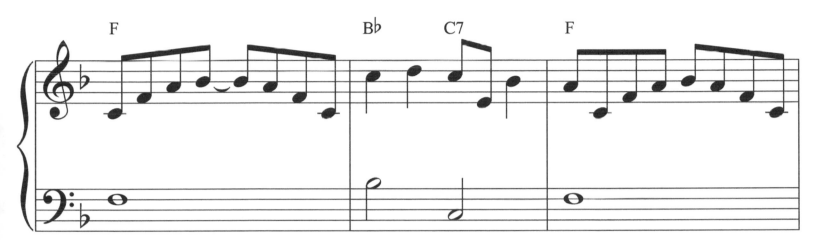

Good - bye Nor - ma Jean. Though I nev - er

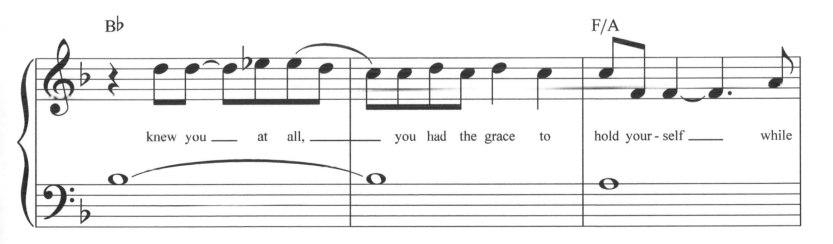

knew you ___ at all, _____ you had the grace to hold your - self _____ while

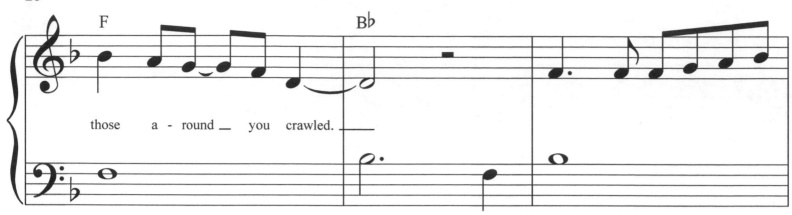

those a - round __ you crawled. ___

Good - bye, Nor - ma Jean, from the young man in the twen - ty - sec - ond row, ___

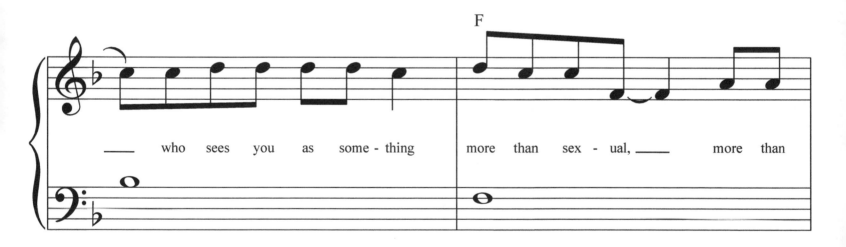

___ who sees you as some - thing more than sex - ual, ___ more than

D.S. al Coda

just our Mar - i - lyn Mon - roe. And it

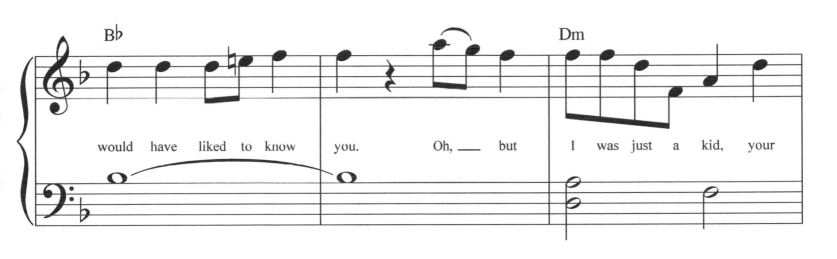

would have liked to know you. Oh, ___ but I was just a kid, your

can - dle burned out long ___ be - fore ___ your

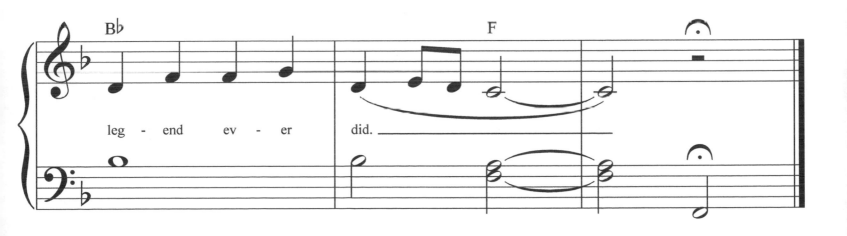

leg - end ev - er did. ___

CROCODILE ROCK

Words and Music by ELTON JOHN
and BERNIE TAUPIN

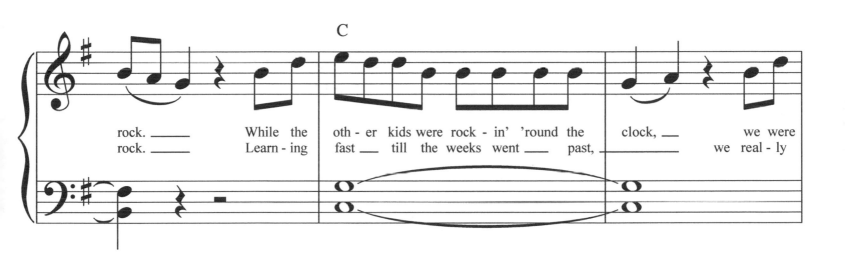

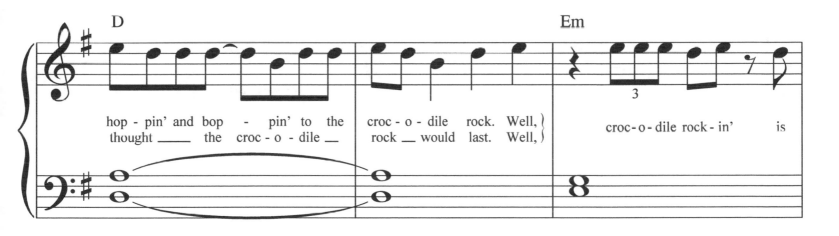

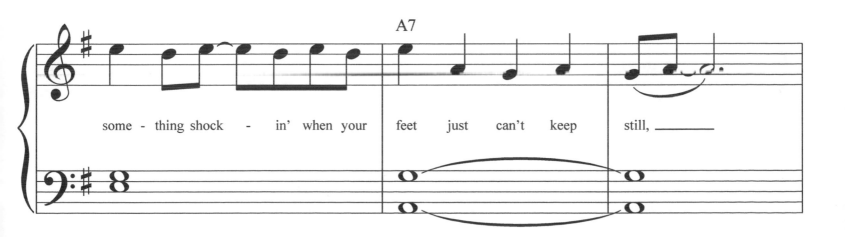

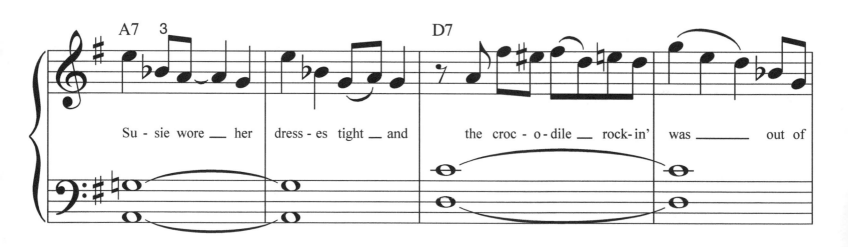

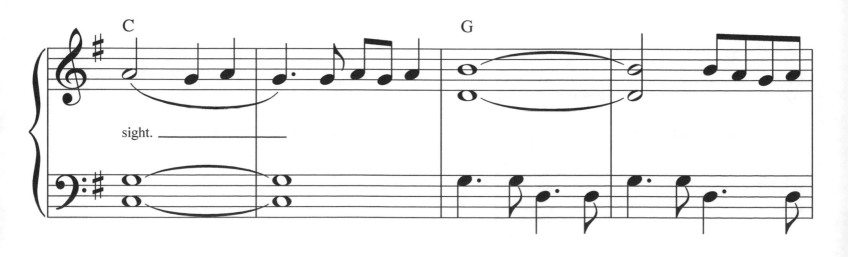

DANIEL

Words and Music by ELTON JOHN
and BERNIE TAUPIN

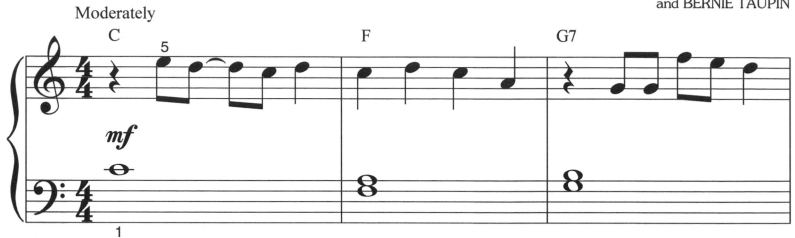

27

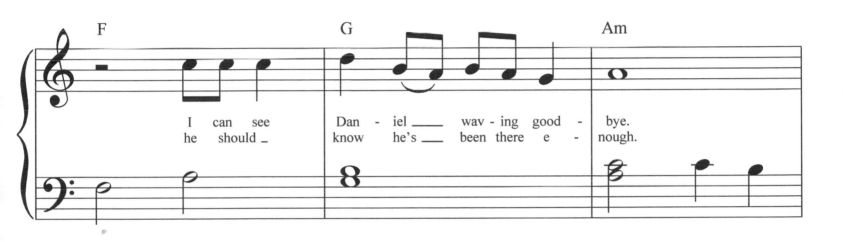

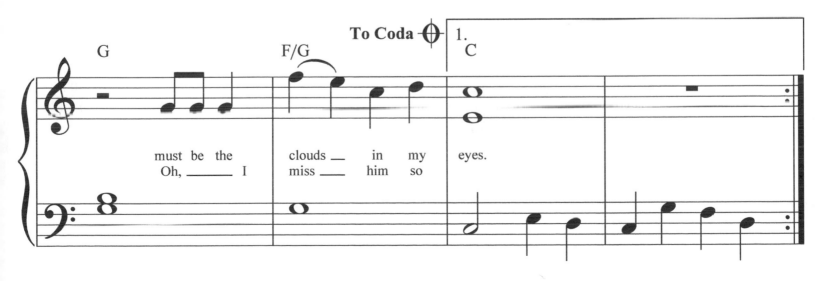

DON'T LET THE SUN GO DOWN ON ME

Words and Music by ELTON JOHN
and BERNIE TAUPIN

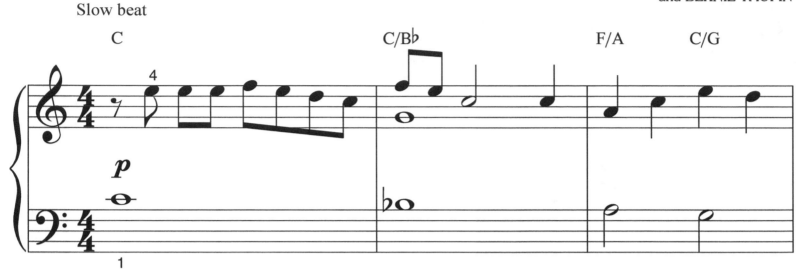

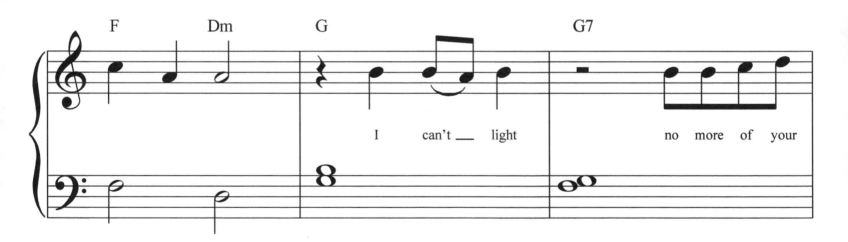

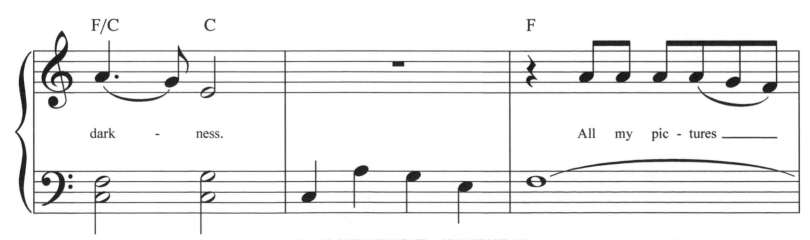

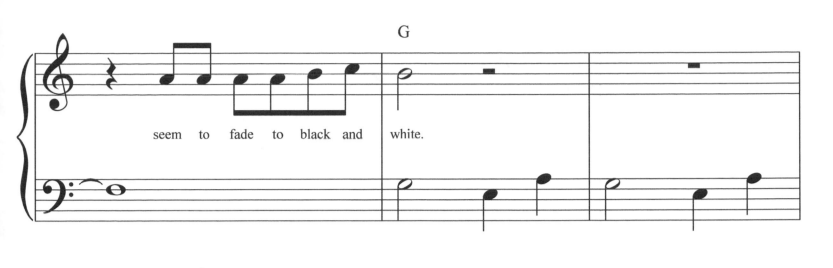

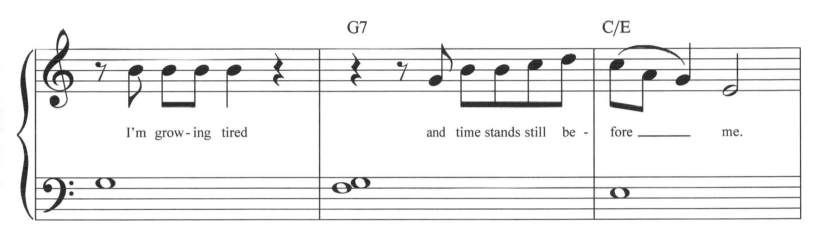

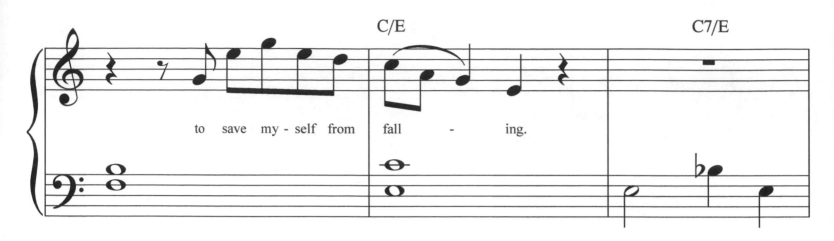

to save my - self from fall - ing.

I took a chance and changed your way of life.

But you mis - read my mean - ing when I

met _____ you. Closed the door

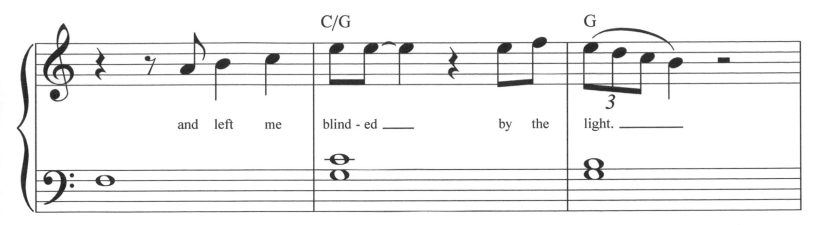

and left me blind - ed _____ by the light. _____

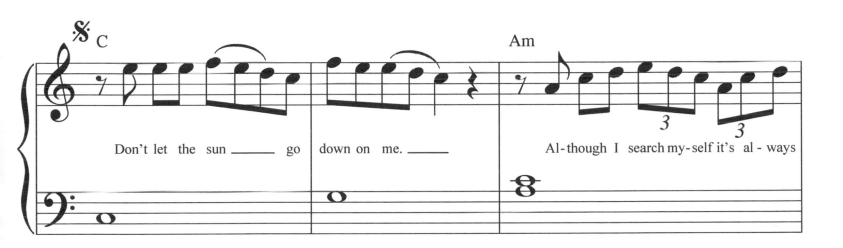

Don't let the sun _____ go down on me. _____ Al-though I search my-self it's al - ways

some - one else I see, _____ I'd just al-low a frag-ment of our life _____ to wan-der

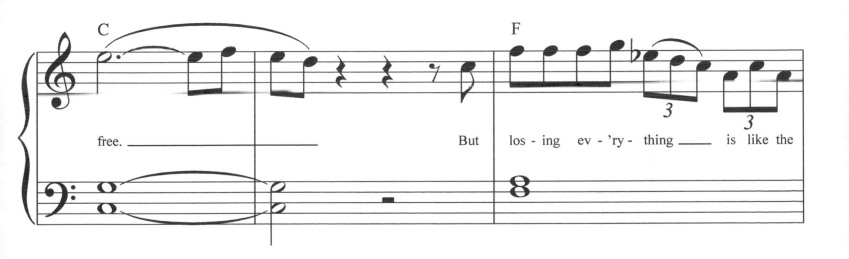

free. _____ But los - ing ev - 'ry - thing _____ is like the

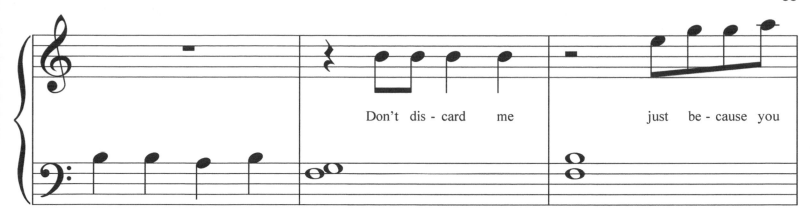

Don't dis - card me   just be - cause you

think I mean you harm. _____   But these cuts I have, _____

_____ oh, they need love   to help them   heal. _____

D.S. al Coda

CODA

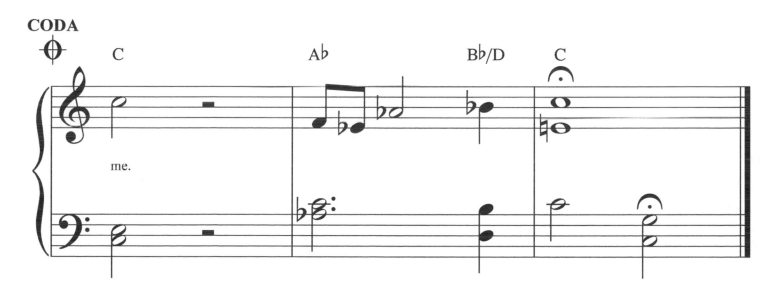

me.

GOODBYE YELLOW BRICK ROAD

Words and Music by ELTON JOHN
and BERNIE TAUPIN

know you can't hold ___ me for - ev - er, I did - n't sign up ___ with you. ___
May - be you'll get ___ a re - place - ment, there's plen - ty like me to be found. __

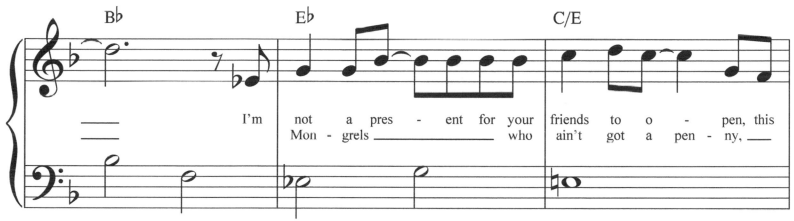

___ I'm not a pres - ent for your friends to o - pen, this
___ Mon - grels ___ who ain't got a pen - ny, ___

boy's too young ___ to be sing - ing ___ the blues. ___
sniff - ing for tid - bits like you ___ on the ground. ___

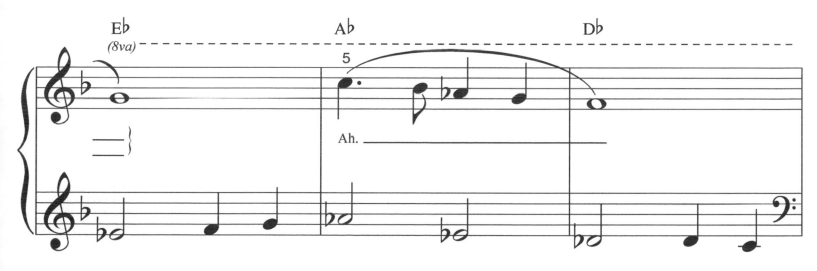

Ah. ___

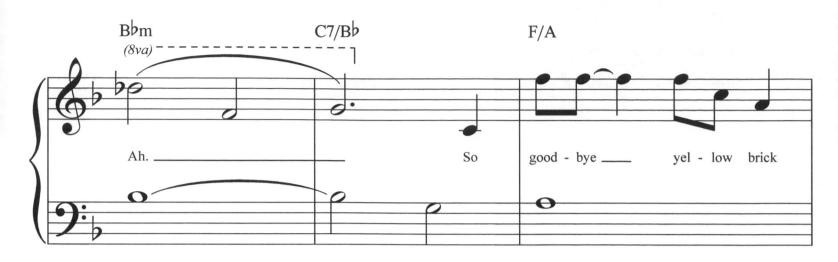

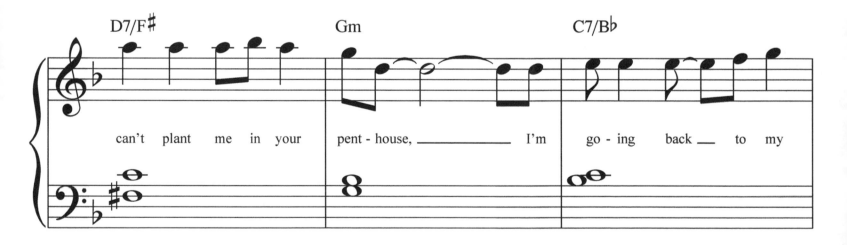

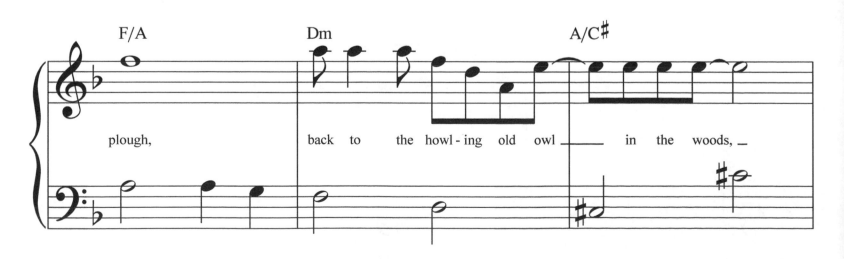

I GUESS THAT'S WHY THEY CALL IT THE BLUES

Words and Music by ELTON JOHN,
BERNIE TAUPIN and DAVEY JOHNSTONE

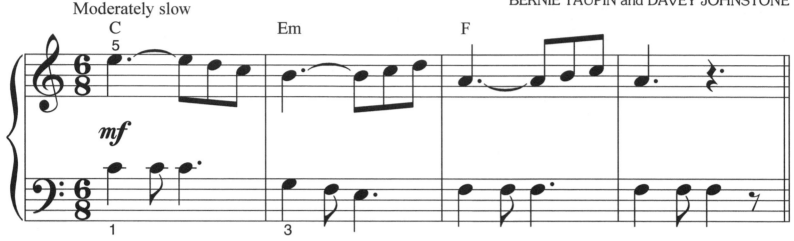

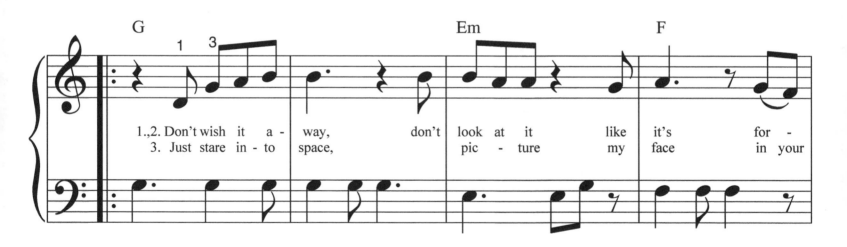

1.,2. Don't wish it a - way, don't look at it like it's for - ev - er.
3. Just stare in - to space, pic - ture my face in your hands. _

Be - tween you and
Live for each

me
sec - ond

I could hon - est - ly say, _____ that
with - out hes - i - ta - tion, and

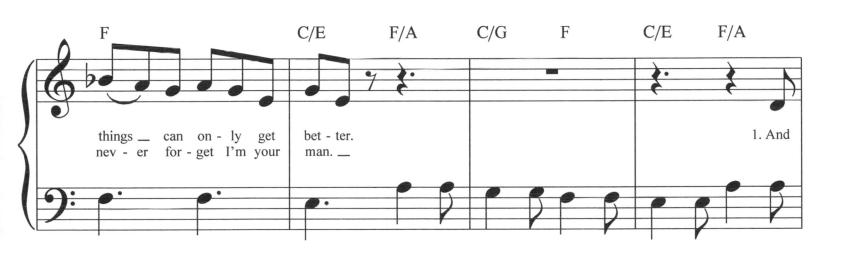

things _ can on - ly get bet - ter. 1. And
nev - er for - get I'm your man. _

while I'm _ a - way girl, bust out the
2.,3. Wait on _ me cry in the

de - mons _ in - side, and it won't _ be long be - fore
night if _ it helps, but more than ev - er I

you and me ____ run, ____ to the place in ____ our
sim - ply love ____ you, ____ more than ____ I

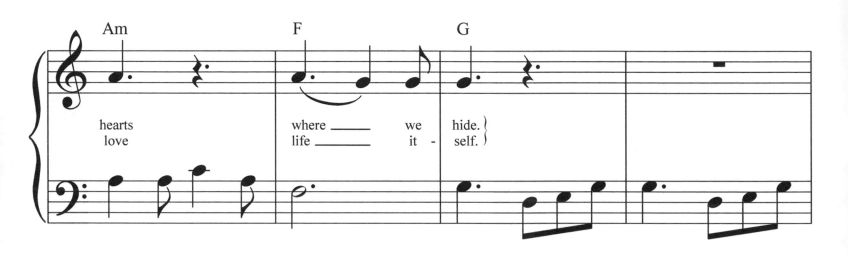

hearts where ____ we hide.
love life ____ it - self.

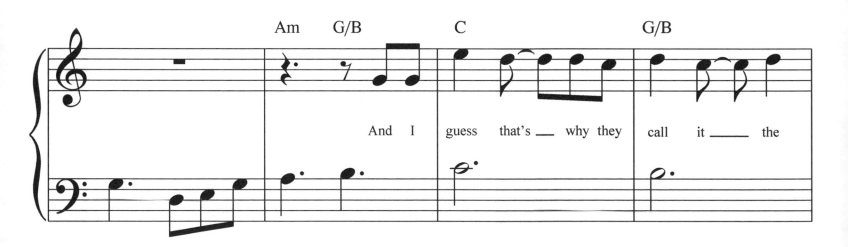

And I guess that's ___ why they call it ____ the

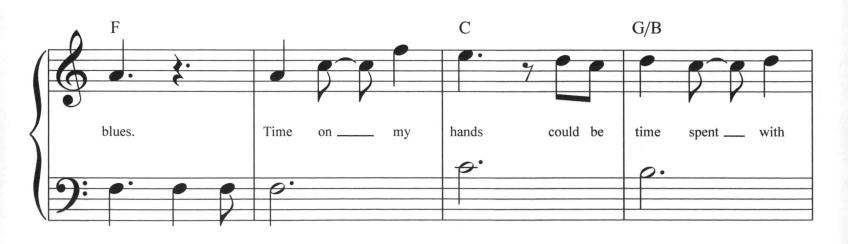

blues. Time on ____ my hands could be time spent ___ with

you, laugh - ing ____ like chil - dren, liv - ing ____ like

lov - ers, roll - ing ____ like thun - der un - der ____ the

cov - ers, and I guess that's ___ why they call ___ it ____ the ___

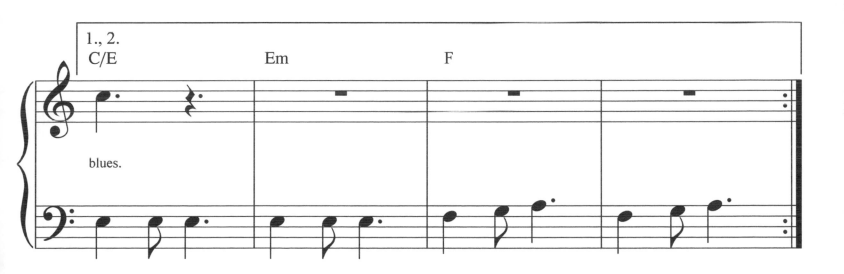

blues.

SAD SONGS
(Say So Much)

Words and Music by ELTON JOHN
and BERNIE TAUPIN

Moderately, with a Blues feel

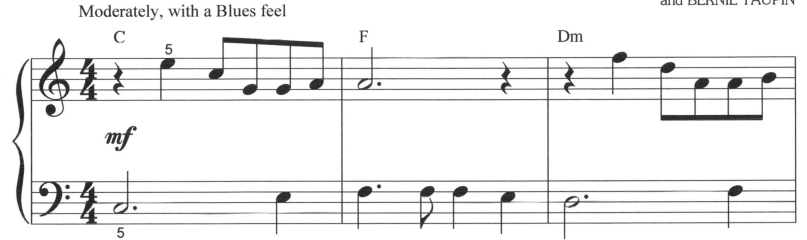

Guess there are   times when, we ___ all ___
If some - one else is   suf - fer - in' ___ e -

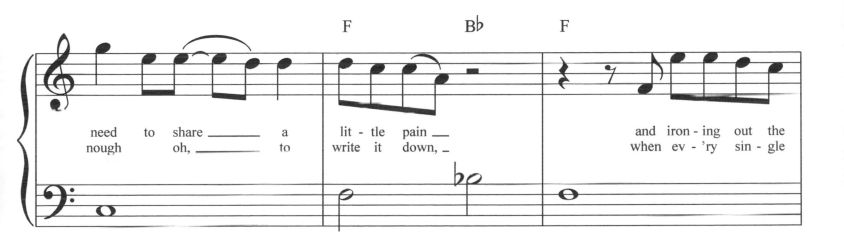

need to share ___ a   lit - tle pain ___   and iron - ing out the
nough   oh, ___ to   write it down, ___   when ev - 'ry sin - gle

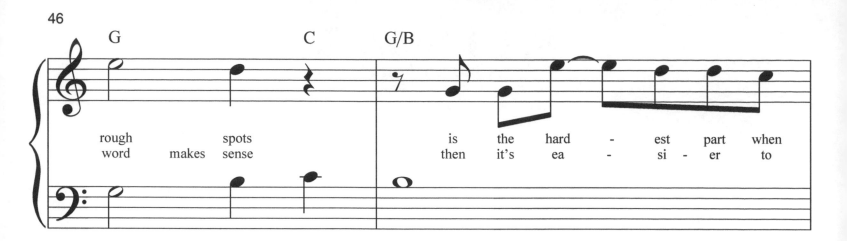

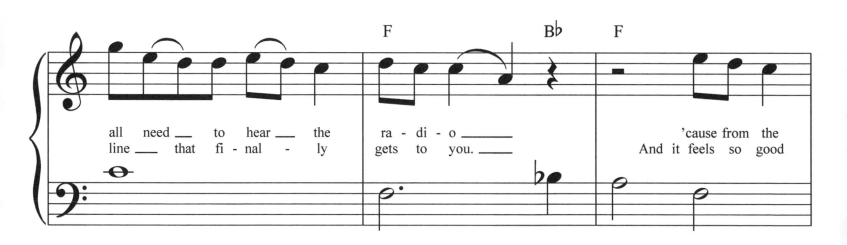

we al-read-y know.
sing _____ the blues.

Turn 'em on, _____ turn 'em on, _____

_____ turn on those sad songs.

When all hope is

gone why don't you tune in and turn _____ them on?

They reach in-to your room, oh, _____ just feel _____ their _____

gen - tle touch. _ When all hope is gone a

To Coda ⊕ | 1. C/E | 2. C

sad song _ says _ so much. much.

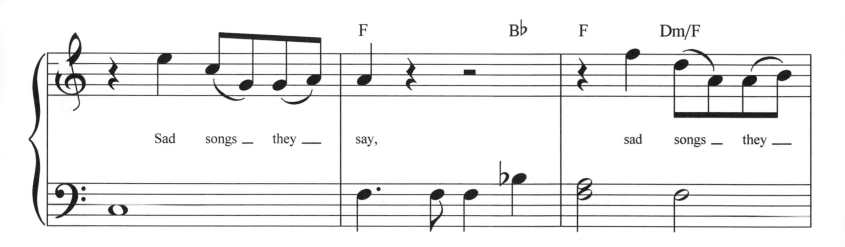

Sad songs _ they _ say, sad songs _ they _

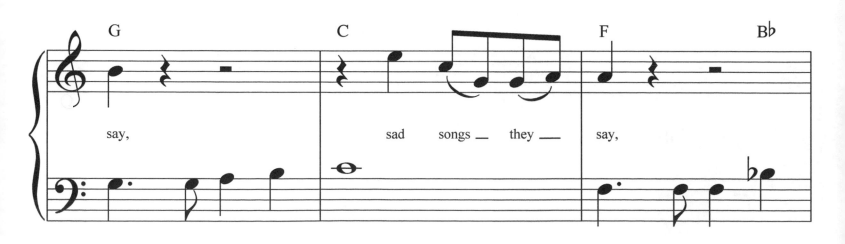

say, sad songs _ they _ say,

D.S. al Coda

I'M STILL STANDING

Words and Music by ELTON JOHN
and BERNIE TAUPIN

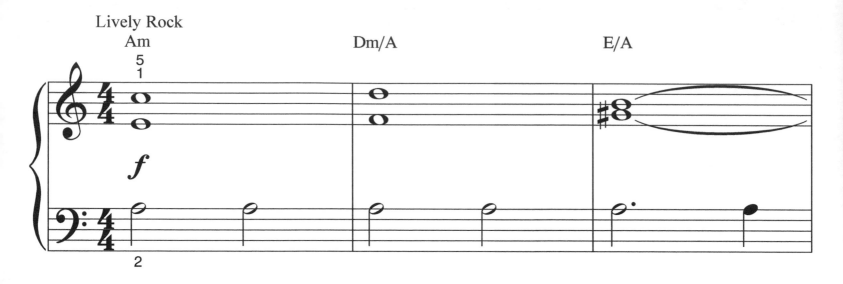

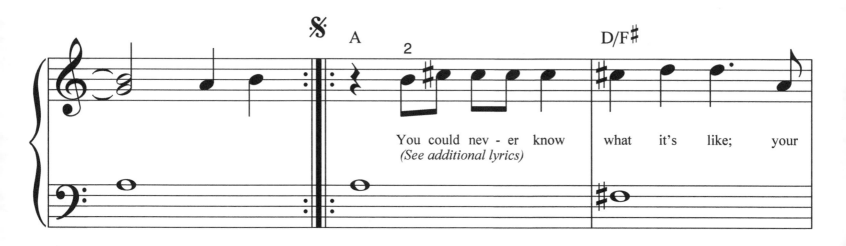

You could nev-er know what it's like; your
(See additional lyrics)

blood like win-ter freez-es just like ice, and there's a cold, lone-ly light that

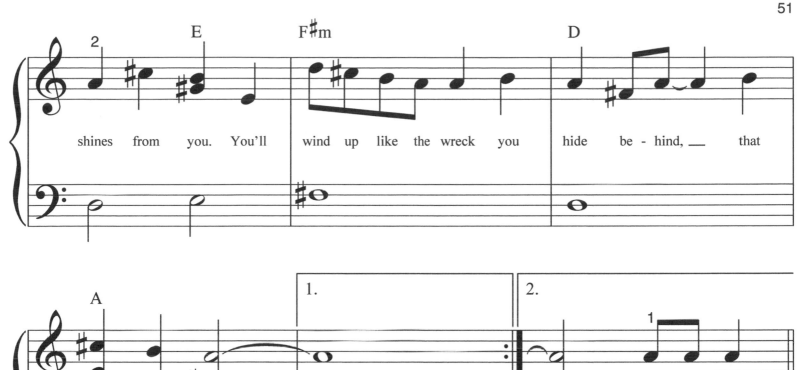

shines from you. You'll wind up like the wreck you hide be - hind, ___ that

mask you use. ___ ___ Don't you know

I'm still stand - in' bet - ter than I ev - er did, ___ ___

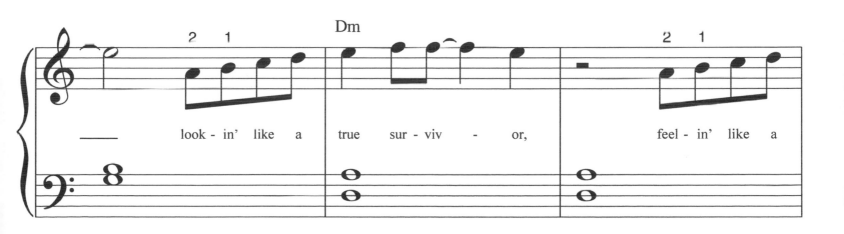

___ look - in' like a true sur - viv - or, feel - in' like a

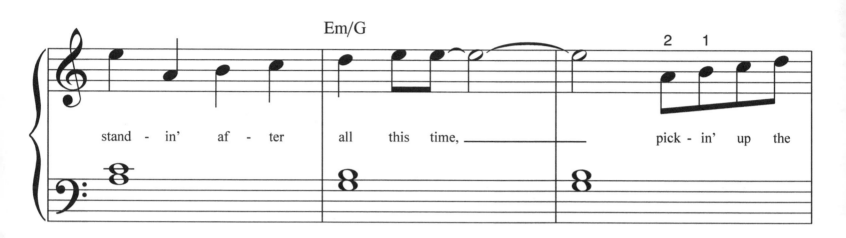

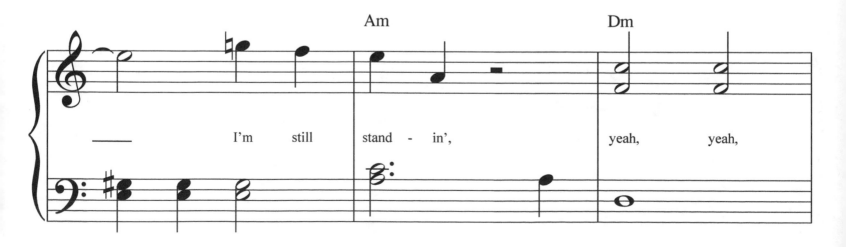

53

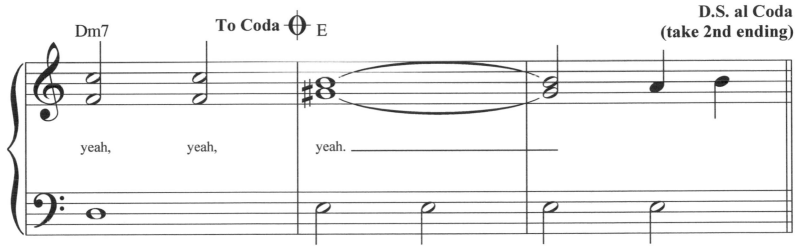

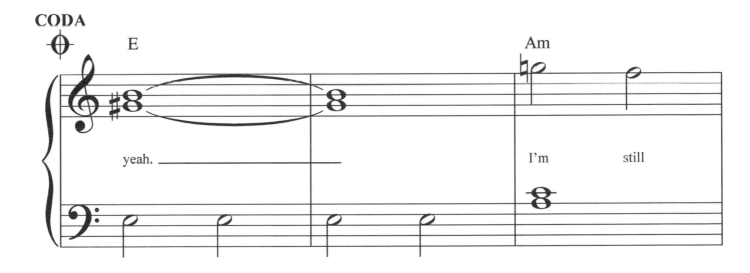

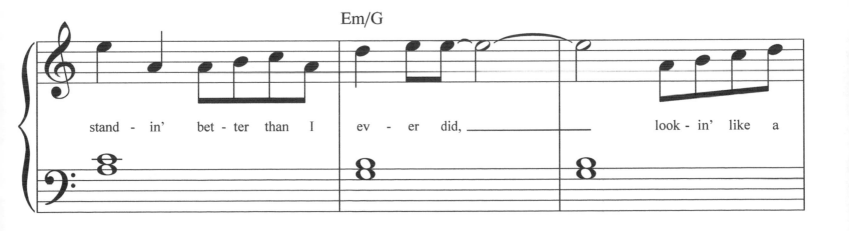

true sur - viv - or, feel - in' like a lit - tle kid. ____

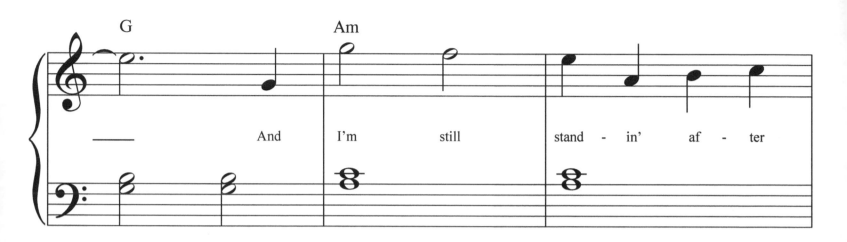

____ And I'm still stand - in' af - ter

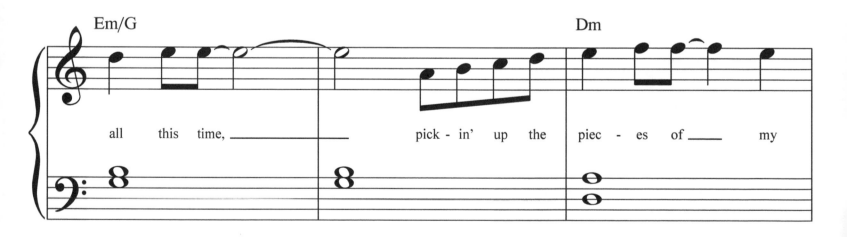

all this time, ____ pick - in' up the piec - es of ____ my

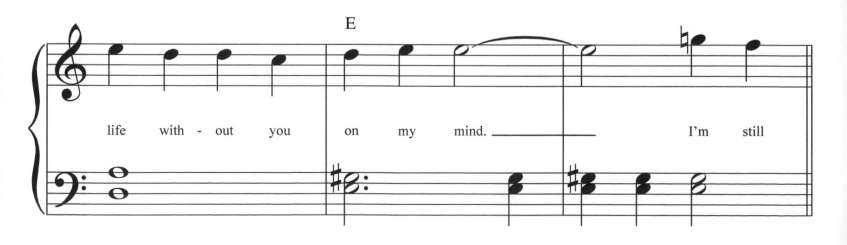

life with - out you on my mind. ____ I'm still

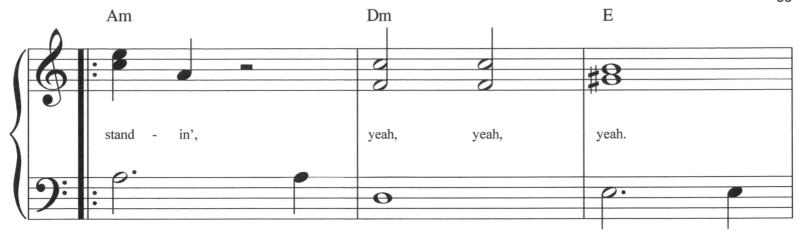

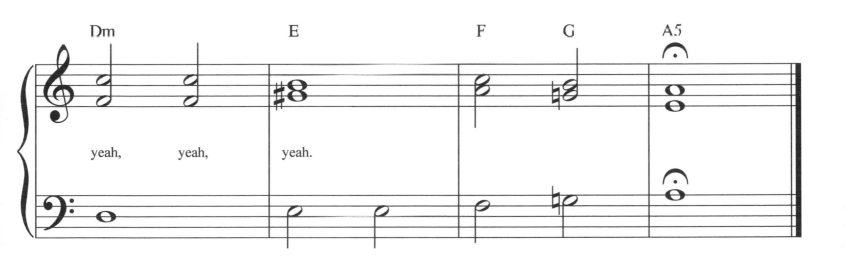

Additional Lyrics

Did you think this fool could never win?
Well, look at me, I'm comin' back again.
I got a taste of love in a simple way,
And if you need to know, while
I'm still standin' you just fade away.

Once I never could hope to win,
You startin' down the road and leavin' me again.
The threats you made were meant to cut me down,
And if our love was just a circus,
You'd be a clown by now.

LEVON

Words and Music by ELTON JOHN
and BERNIE TAUPIN

MONA LISAS AND MAD HATTERS

Words and Music by ELTON JOHN
and BERNIE TAUPIN

In a slow two

Now I know ___ it's got a lot of songs
This Broadway's got, ___ "Span - ish Har -

- lem" are not just pret - ty words ___ to say. ___
to sing. If I know the tunes I might join in. ___

I thought I knew, ___
I go my way a - lone, ___

but now I know ___ that rose trees
grow my own. My own trees seeds

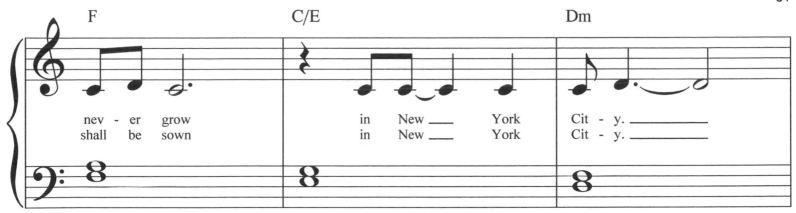

never grow / shall be sown — in New ___ York / in New ___ York — Cit - y. ___ / Cit - y. ___

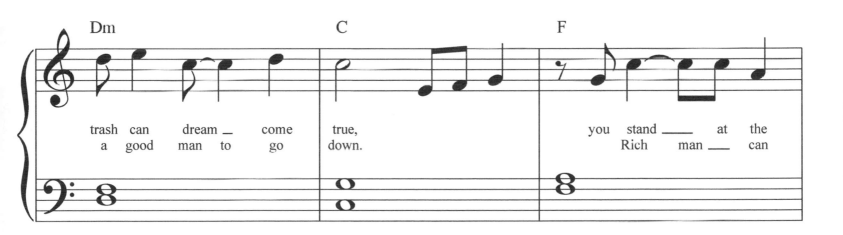

Un - til ___ you've / Sub - way's ___ no — seen / way — this / for

trash can dream ___ come / a good man to go — true, / down. — you stand ___ at the / Rich man ___ can

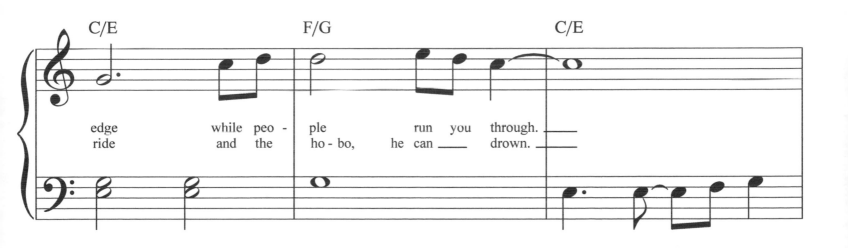

edge / ride — while peo - / and the — ple / ho - bo, — run you through. ___ / he can ___ drown. ___

And I thank ___ the Lord ___ ___ there's peo - ple out there ___ like you. ___
And I thank ___ the Lord ___ for the peo - ple ___ I have found. ___

___ I thank the Lord there's peo - ple out there like
I thank the Lord for the peo - ple I ___ have

you. ___
found. ___

While Mo - na Li - sas and Mad Hat - ters, sons of bank -

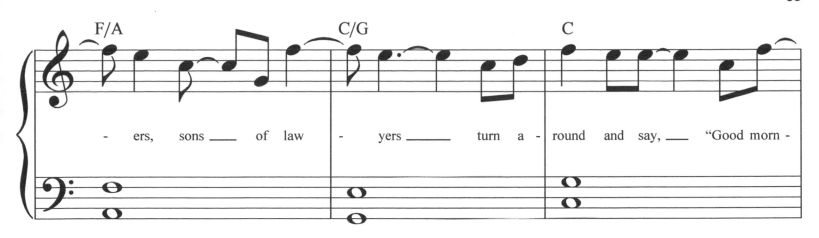

- ers, sons __ of law - yers __ turn a - round and say, __ "Good morn -

- ing" to __ the night. __ For un -

less they see __ the sky, but they can't and that is why, __

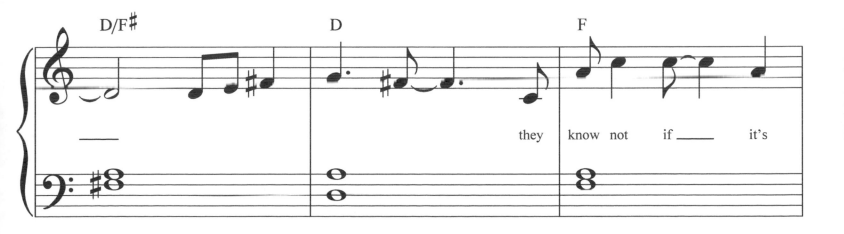

__ they know not if __ it's

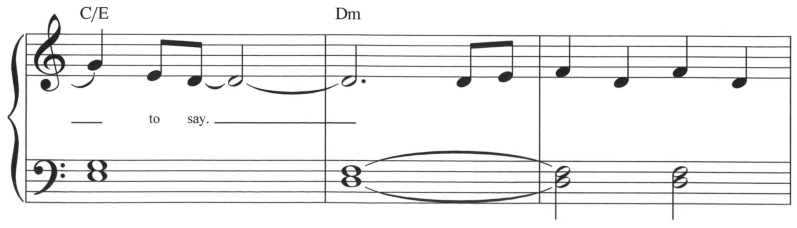

65

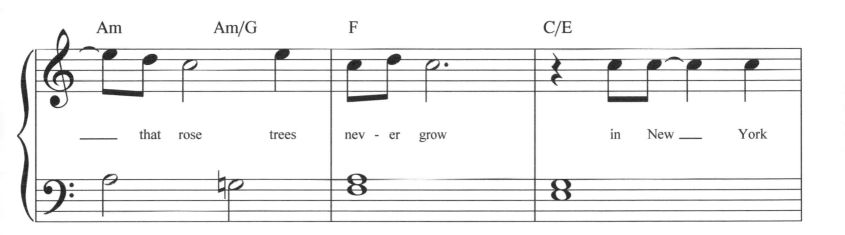

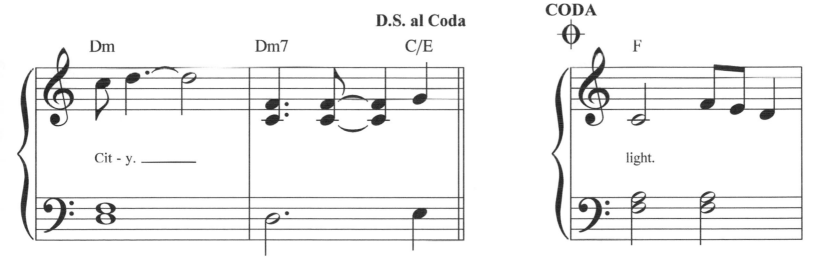

PHILADELPHIA FREEDOM

Words and Music by ELTON JOHN
and BERNIE TAUPIN

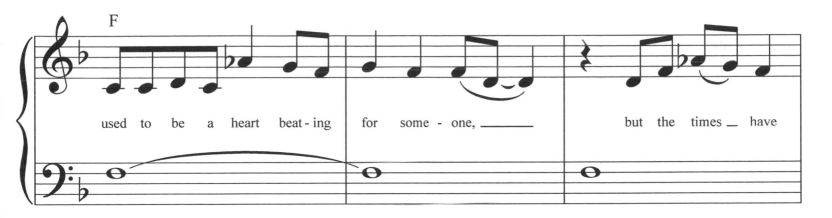

used to be a heart beat-ing for some - one, _____ but the times _ have

changed. The less I say _ the more _ my work gets

done. 'Cause I live and breathe _ this

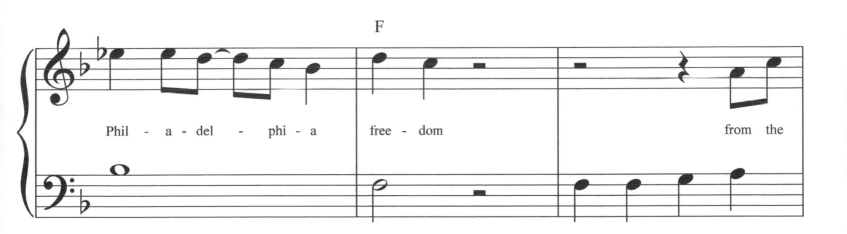

Phil - a - del - phi - a free - dom from the

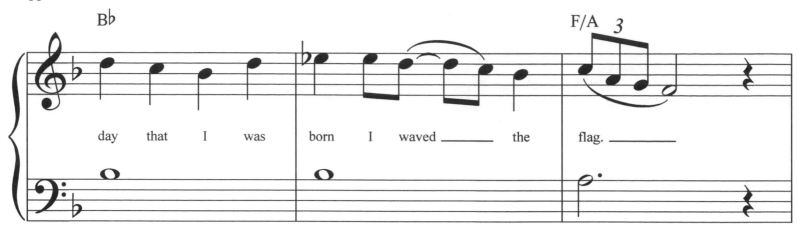

day that I was born I waved _____ the flag. _____

Phil - a - del - phia free - dom took me knee - high to a

man. _____ Yeah! Gave me peace of mind my

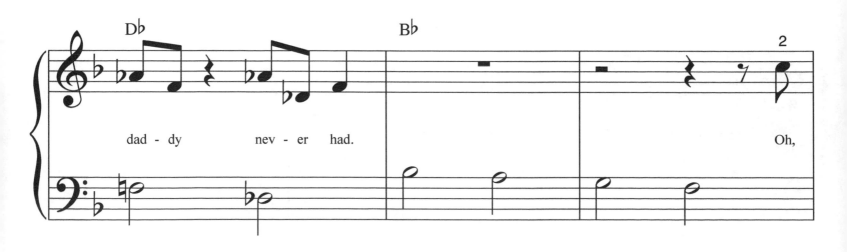

dad - dy nev - er had. Oh,

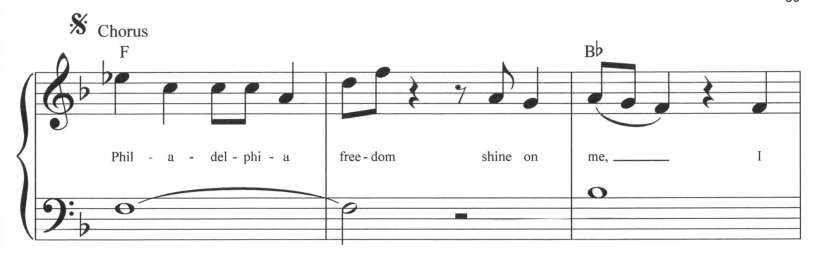

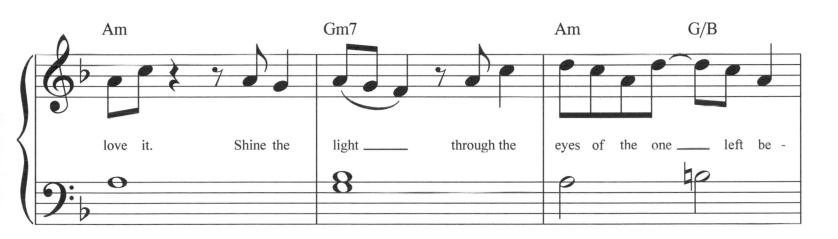

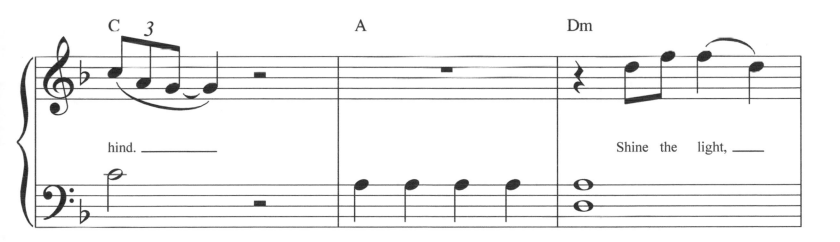

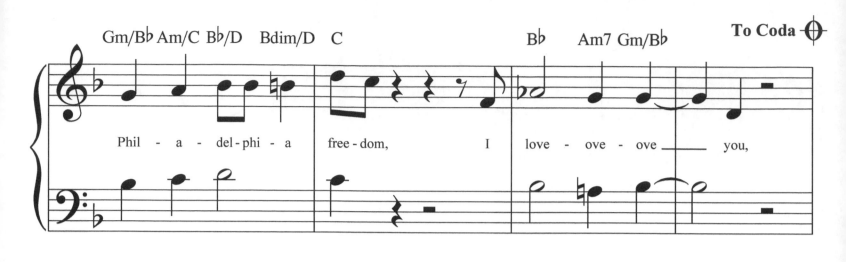

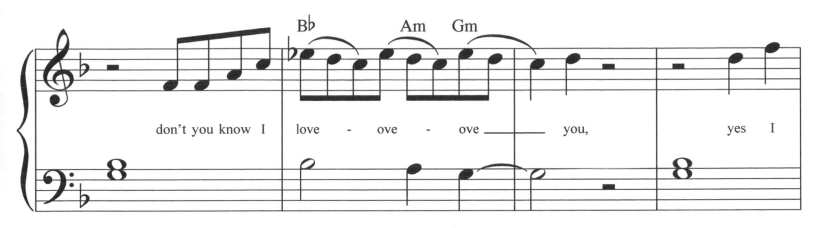

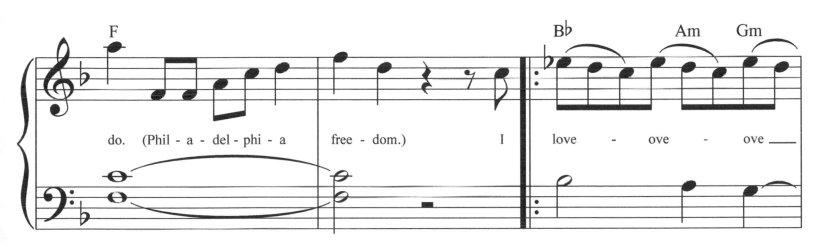

Additional Lyrics

If you choose to, you can live your life alone.
Some people choose the city,
Some others choose the good old family home.
I like living easy without family ties,
'Til the whippoorwill of freedom zapped me
Right between the eyes.
Chorus

ROCKET MAN
(I Think It's Gonna Be a Long Long Time)

Words and Music by ELTON JOHN
and BERNIE TAUPIN

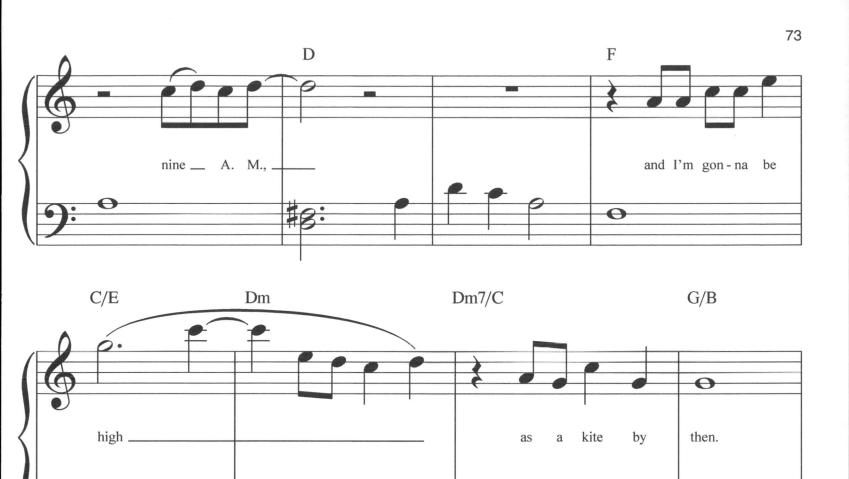

D   F

nine __ A. M., __   and I'm gon-na be

C/E   Dm   Dm7/C   G/B

high _____   as   a   kite   by   then.

G   G/B   G/D   Am

I   miss __   the

D   Am

earth so much,   I   miss __ my wife. __   It's

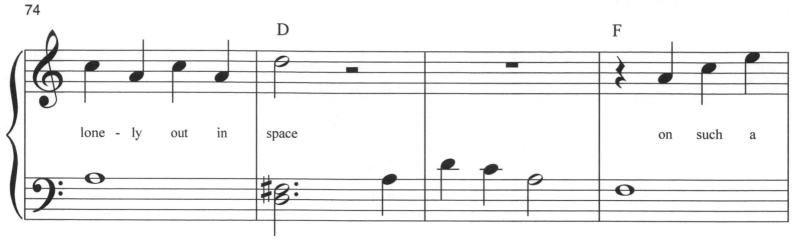

lone - ly out in space

on such a

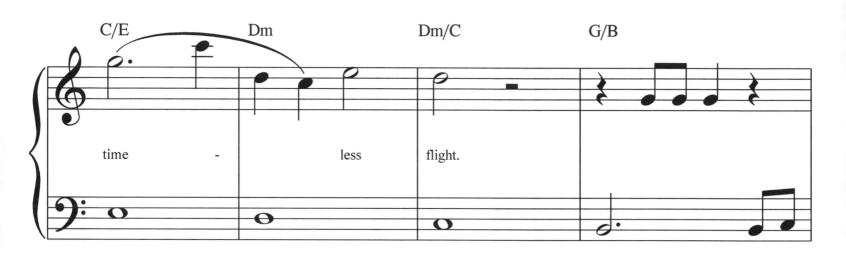

time - less flight.

And I think it's gon-na

be a long, long time till touch - down brings me 'round a - gain to find I'm not the

man they think I am at home. Oh, no, no, no, I'm a rock-et man. _____

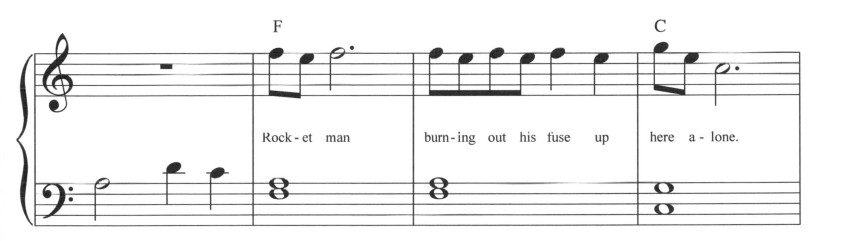

Rock-et man burn-ing out his fuse up here a-lone.

To Coda ⊕

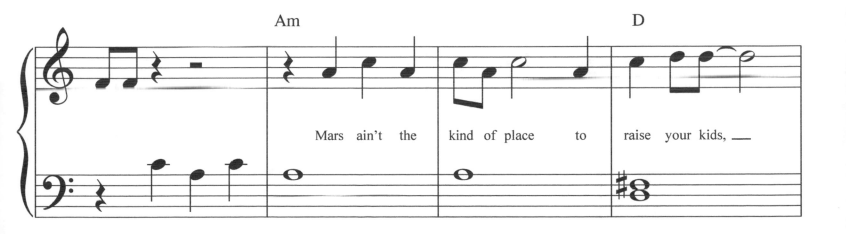

Mars ain't the kind of place to raise your kids, _____

in fact, it's cold ___ as hell.

And there's no one there to raise _____ them

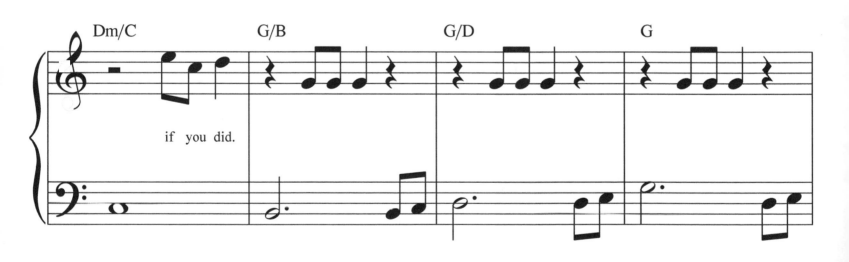

if you did.

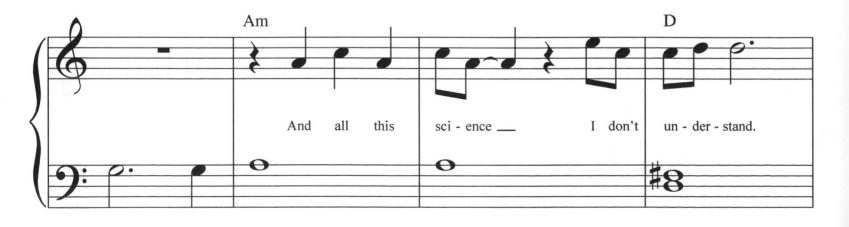

And all this sci - ence ___ I don't un - der - stand.

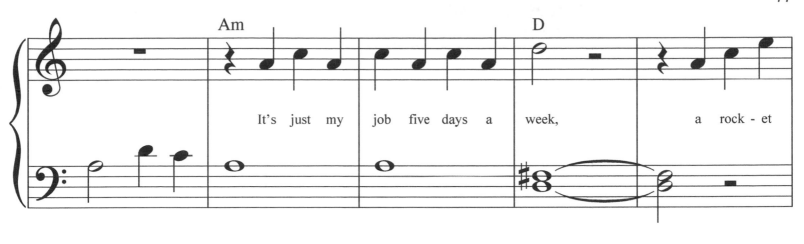

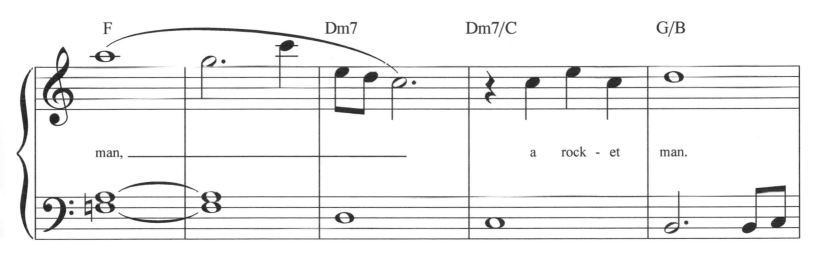

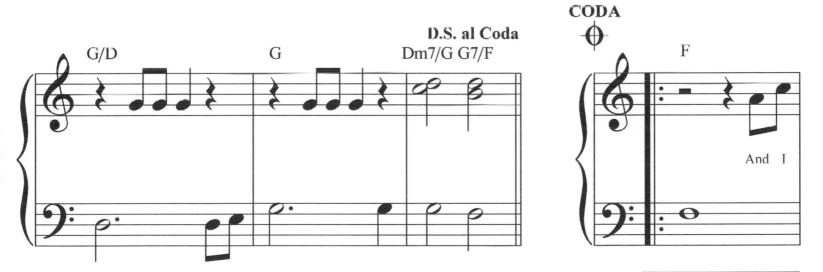

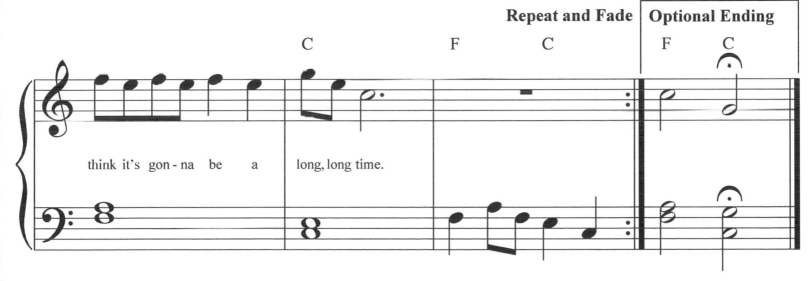

SATURDAY NIGHT'S ALRIGHT
(For Fighting)

Words and Music by ELTON JOHN
and BERNIE TAUPIN

beer. My old man's drunk-er than a bar-rel full of mon-keys and my

old la - dy she don't care. My sis - ter looks cute in her

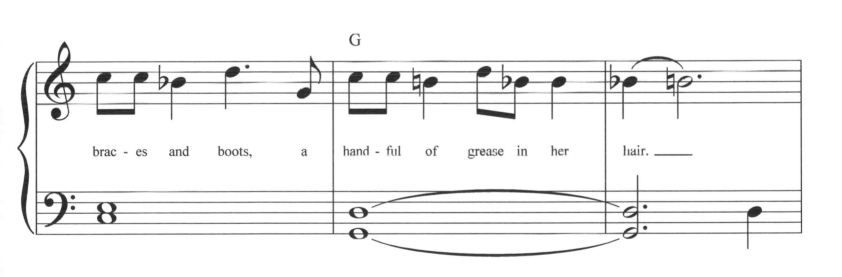

brac - es and boots, a hand - ful of grease in her hair. _____

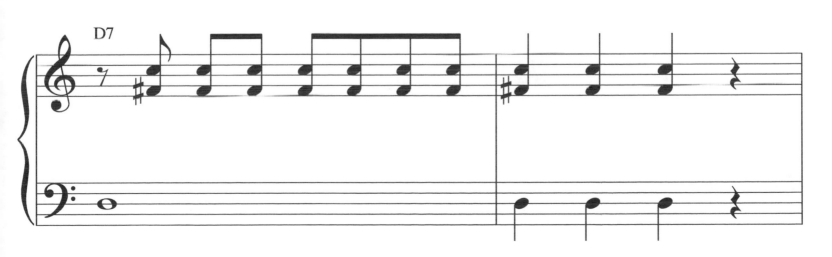

So don't give us none of your ag - gra - va - tion, we've had it with your dis - ci -

pline. __ Oh, Sat - ur-day night's __ al - right for fight - in', get a lit - tle ac - tion __ in, __

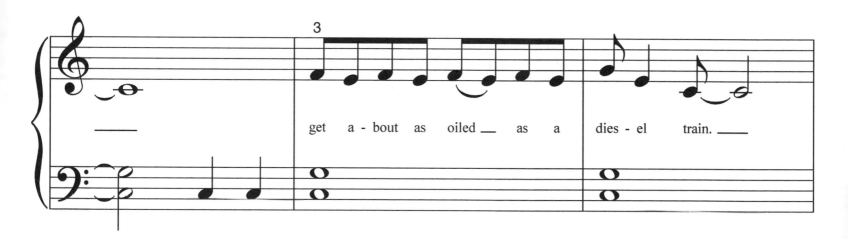

__ get a - bout as oiled __ as a dies - el train. __

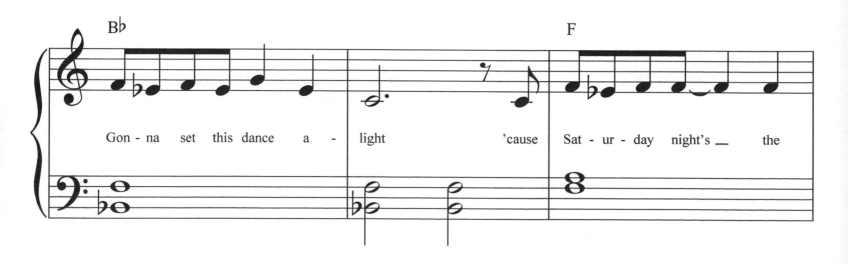

Gon - na set this dance a - light 'cause Sat - ur-day night's __ the

night I like. _____ Sat - ur - day night's _ al - right, al - right, al -

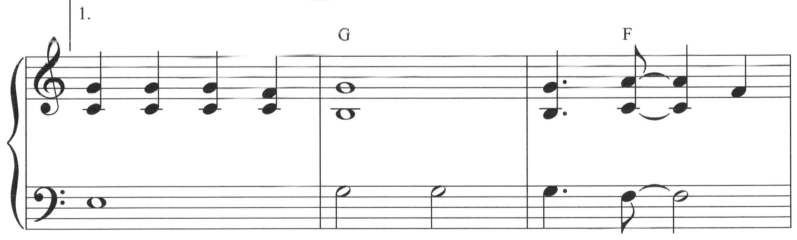

right. _____ Ooh. _____

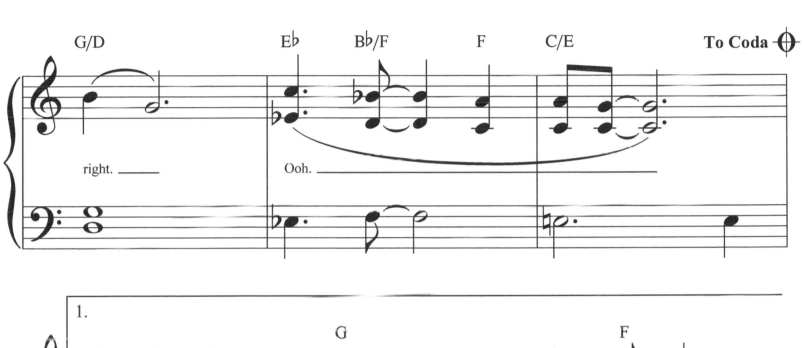

Well, they're

Additional Lyrics

Well, they're packed pretty tight in here tonight.
I'm looking for a dolly to see me right.
I may use a little muscle to get what I need,
I may sink a little drink and shout out she's with me.
A couple of sounds that I really like are the
Sound of a switch-blade and a motor bike.
I'm a juvenile product of the working class
Whose best friend floats in the bottom of a glass.
Ooh.

SOMEONE SAVED MY LIFE TONIGHT

Words and Music by ELTON JOHN
and BERNIE TAUPIN

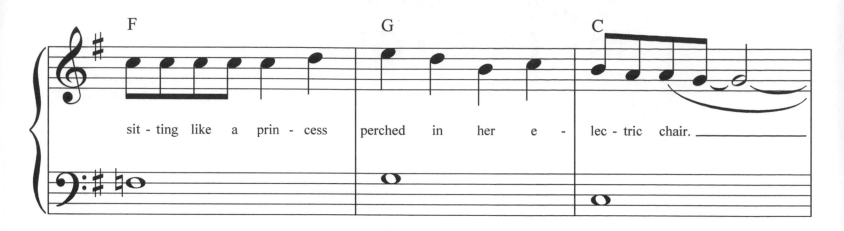

sit - ting like a prin - cess perched in her e - lec - tric chair. _____

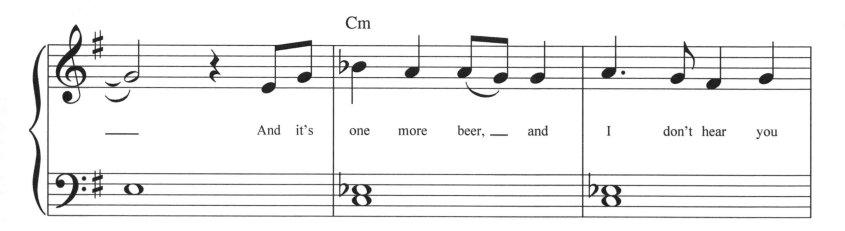

_____ And it's one more beer, ___ and I don't hear you

an - y - more. _____ We've all gone cra - zy

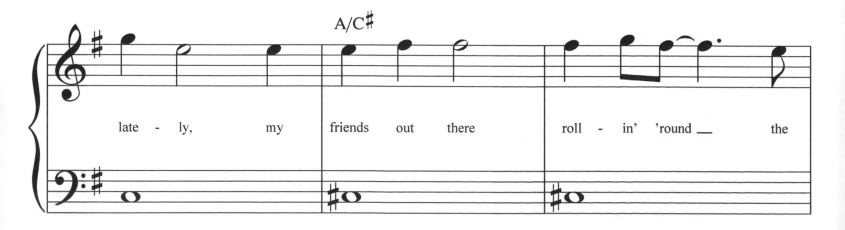

late - ly, my friends out there roll - in' 'round ___ the

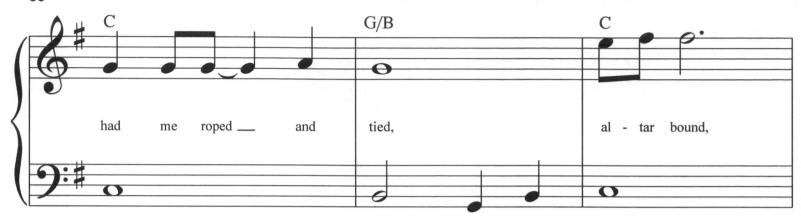

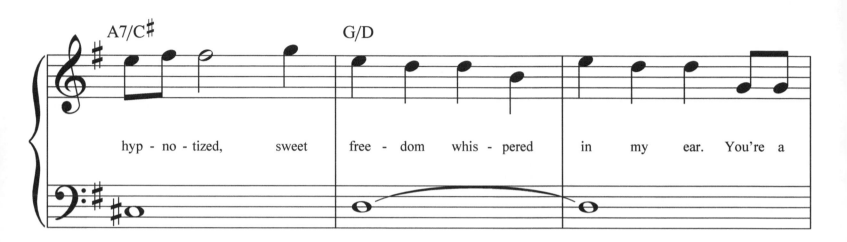

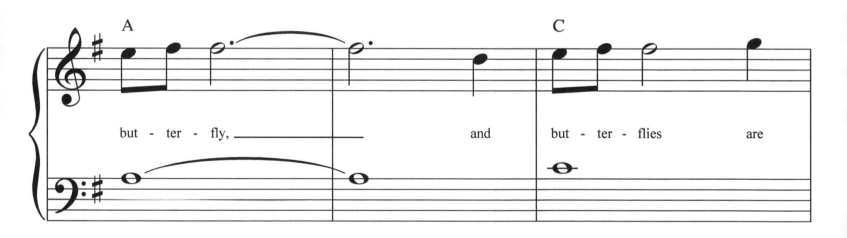

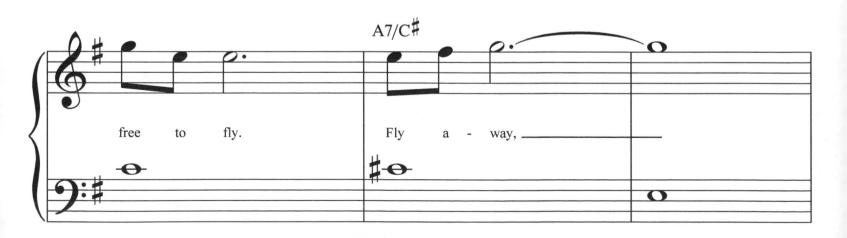

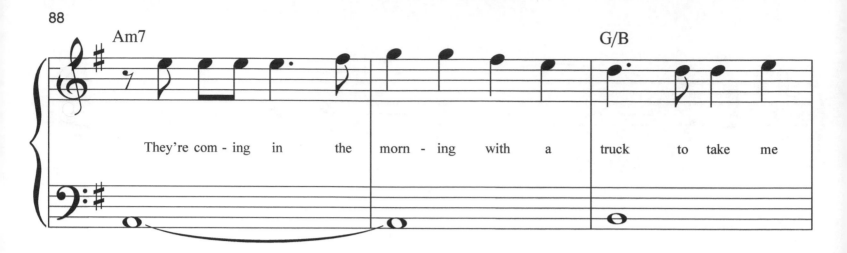

They're com - ing in the morn - ing with a truck to take me

home. Some - one saved my life to - night, ___

some - one saved my life to - night, _____ some - one saved my

life to - night, ___ some - one saved my life to - night, _____

some-one saved my life to-night. So save your strength and run the field you

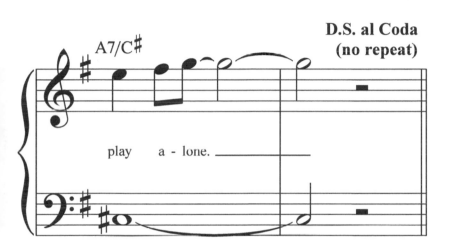

D.S. al Coda
(no repeat)

play a-lone.

CODA

Some-one saved, some-one

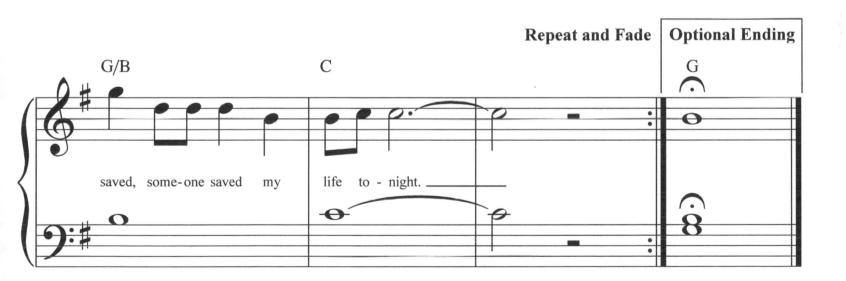

Repeat and Fade | **Optional Ending**

saved, some-one saved my life to-night.

Additional Lyrics

I never realized the passing hours
Of evening showers,
A slip noose hanging in my darkest dreams.
I'm strangled by your haunted social scene
Just a pawn out-played by a dominating queen.
It's four-o-clock in the morning
Damn it!
Listen to me good.
I'm sleeping with myself tonight.
Saved in time, thank God my music's still alive.

Sorry Seems To Be The Hardest Word

Words and Music by ELTON JOHN
and BERNIE TAUPIN

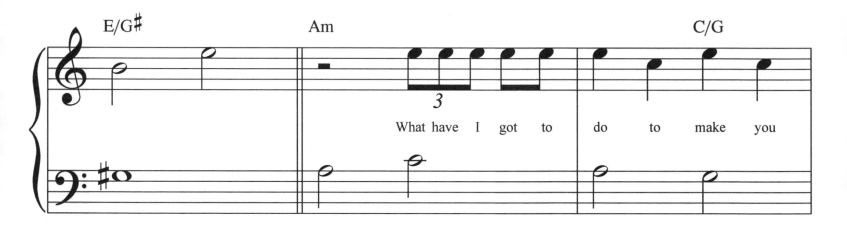

What have I got to do to make you

love me?   What have I got to

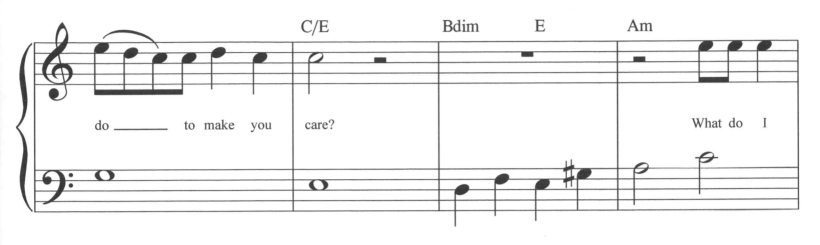

to _____ be heard?

C/E   Bdim   E   Am

What do I

Dm7/F

say when it's all o - ver?

G/B

Sor - ry   seems to

G

be the hard - est word.

C/E   G   F/A

It's sad, _____

E/G♯

so sad. _____

C/G

It's a sad, sad

F♯m7

sit - u - a - tion

Dm

and it's get - ting

more and more ab - surd.   It's sad, _____

so sad. _____   Why can't we   talk it o - ver?   Oh, it seems to me _

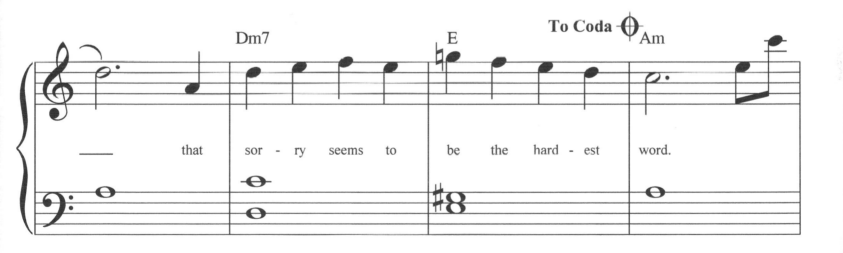

To Coda

_____   that   sor - ry seems to   be   the   hard - est   word.

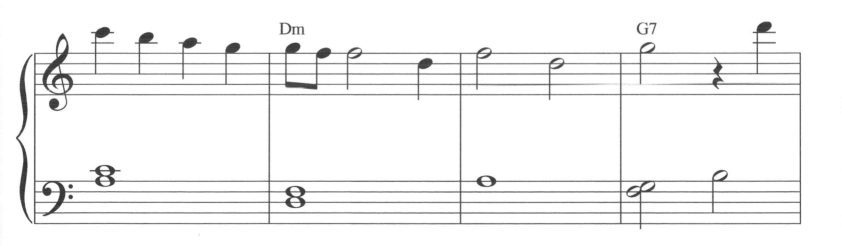

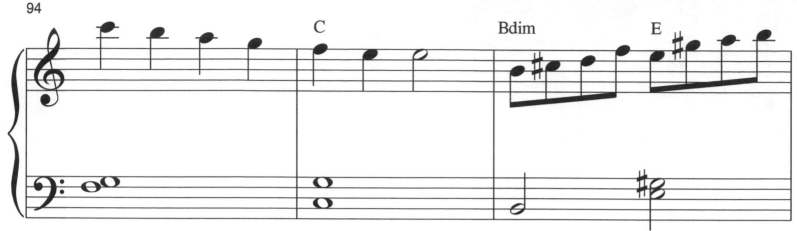

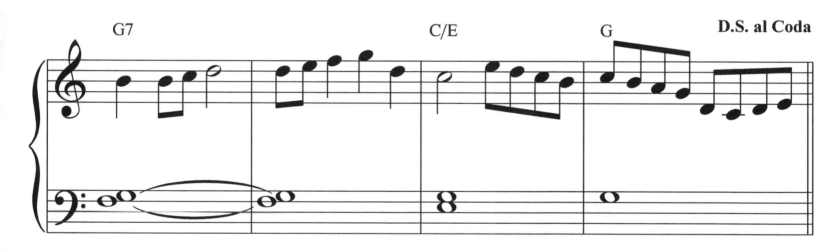

D.S. al Coda

word. What do I do to make you love me?

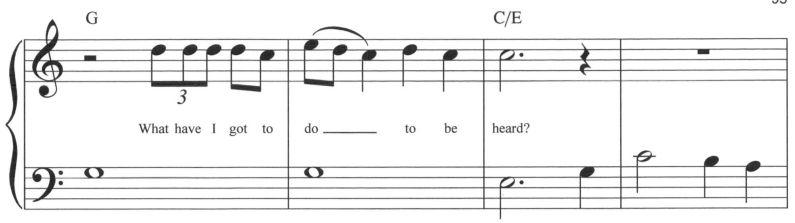

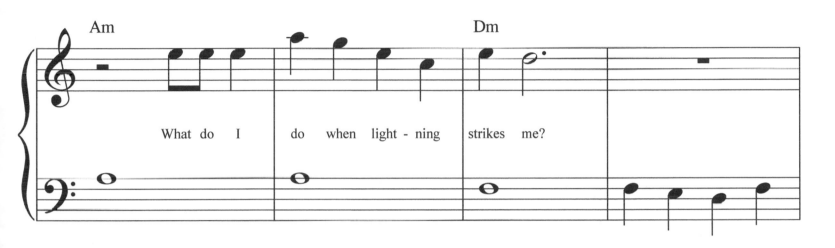

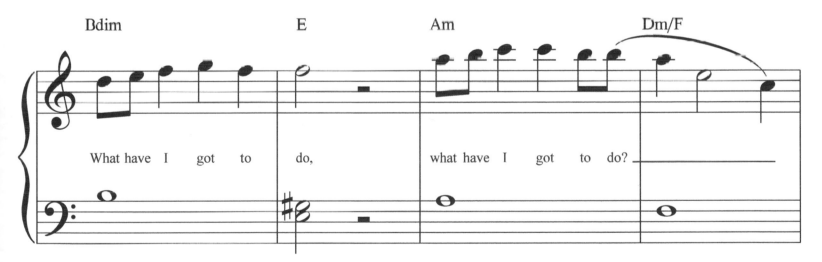

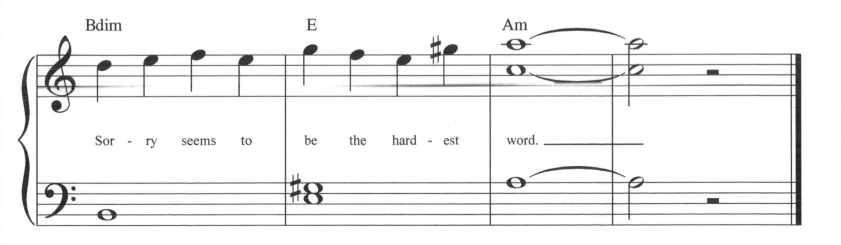

TINY DANCER

Words and Music by ELTON JOHN
and BERNIE TAUPIN

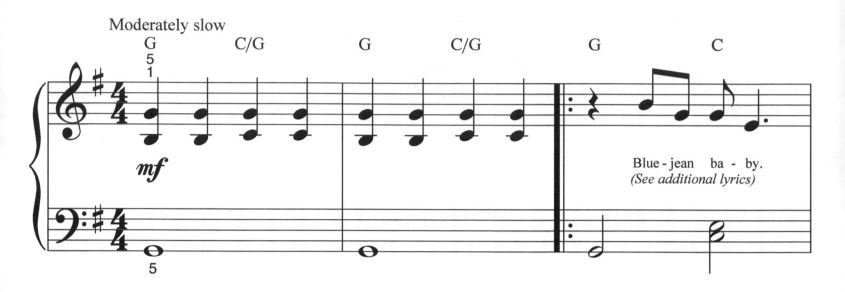

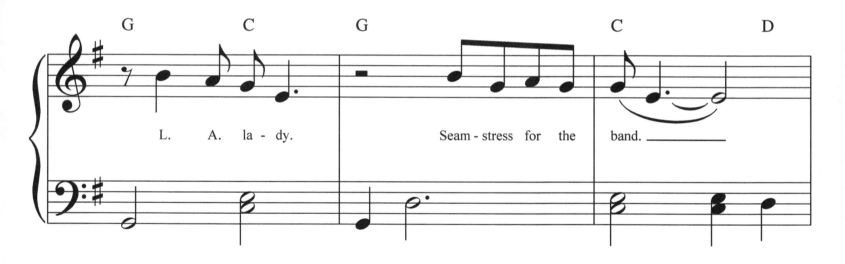

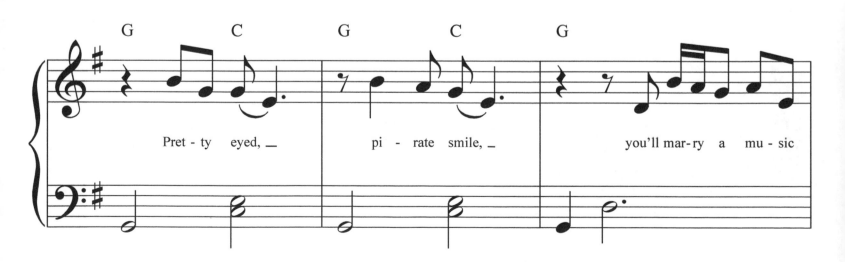

Additional Lyrics

Jesus freaks out in the street
Handing tickets out for God.
Turning back, she just laughs.
The boulevard is not that bad.
Piano man, he makes his stand
In the auditorium.
Looking on, she sings the songs.
The word she knows, the tune she hums.

YOUR SONG

Words and Music by ELTON JOHN
and BERNIE TAUPIN

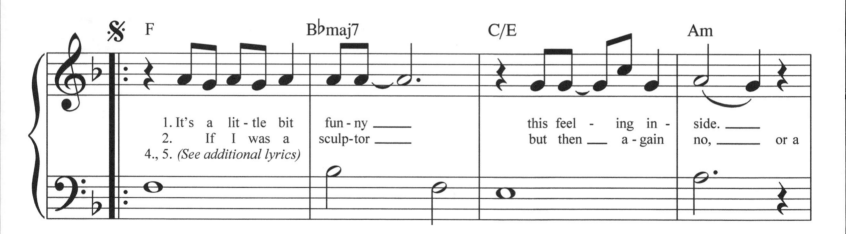

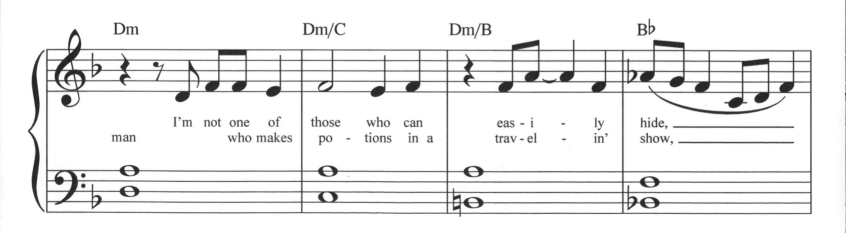

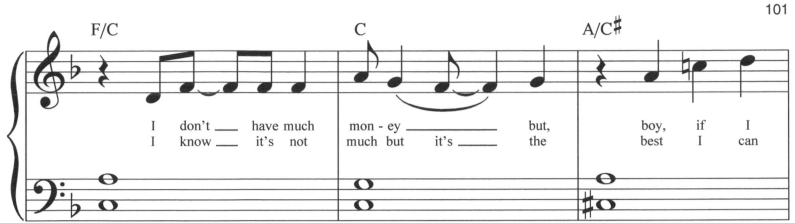

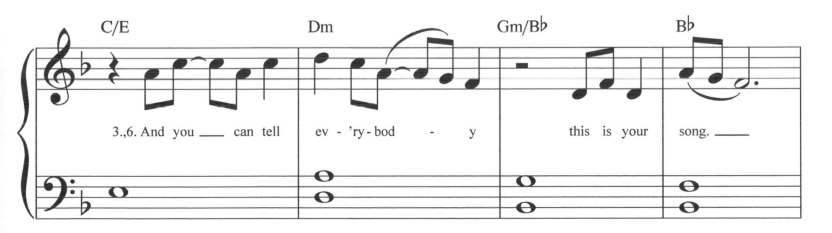

102

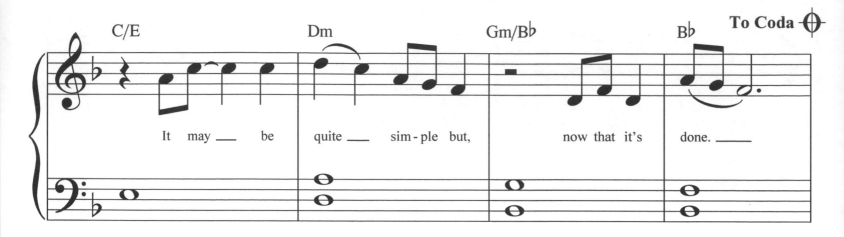

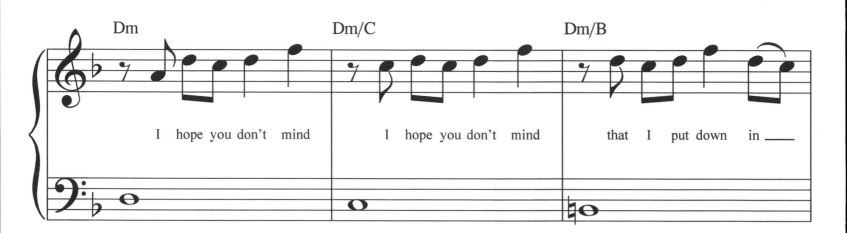

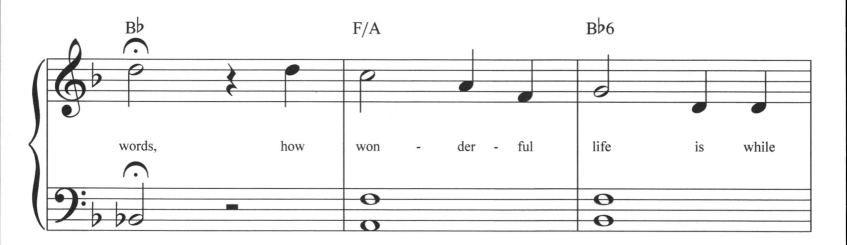

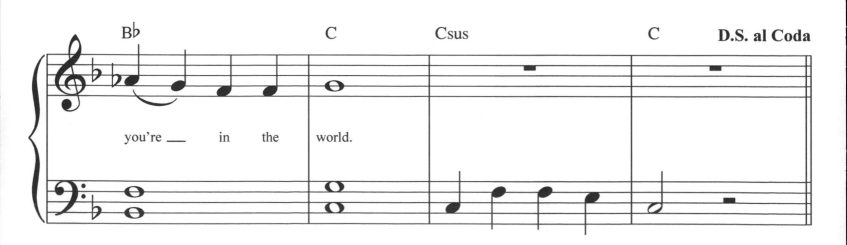

CODA

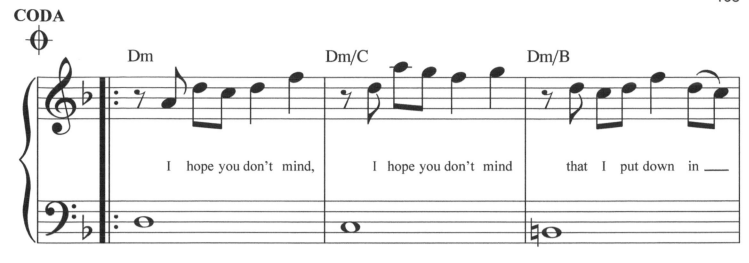

Dm   **Dm/C**   **Dm/B**

I hope you don't mind,   I hope you don't mind   that I put down in ___

B♭6   **F/A**   **B♭6**   **1.** **B♭**

words,   how   won - der - ful   life   is   while   you're ___ in   the

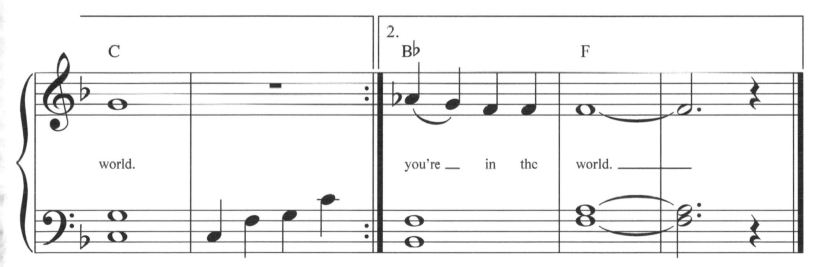

C   **2.** **B♭**   **F**

world.   you're ___ in the world. ___

Additional Lyrics

4. I sat on a roof and kicked off the moss.
   Well, a few of the versions, well, they've got me quite cross.
   But the sun's been quite kind while I wrote this song.
   It's for people like you that keep it turned on.

5. So excuse me forgetting but these things I do.
   You see I've forgotten if they're green or they're blue.
   Anyway the thing is what I really mean,
   Yours are the sweetest eyes I've ever seen.